T

T

Ess   st
for   ship'

4th

Published by Garuda Publications and available from:

Garuda Publications
41 Beech Close
Walton-on-Thames
Surrey KT12 5RQ, UK
www.GarudaPublications.com

Cover design by Goran J. Tomic

ISBN 978-1-9996650-0-5

Edited by Andrew Thompson
Printed by Page Bros Group, Norwich, UK

Free Online Interactive E-learning book and Practice Tests

Create an account at *Training.GarudaPublications.com.* Then use the enrollment
key **Garuda2017** to gain free access to the Interactive E-learning book and
practice tests - currently for up to 5 days. *Garuda Publications reserves the right
to vary the free term and enrollment keys without prior notice.*

Contents

Introduction

To settle permanently in the United Kingdom (UK) or be granted British Citizenship most people now have to pass 'The Life in the UK Test'. The test is taken some 140,000 times a year.

The pass rates for the current test is approximately 70%. So, about seven in every ten candidates pass.

This handbook is intended to help candidates pass the Life in the UK test first time. The 'official study materials' that the test is based on are reproduced in full in this book so no other study guide should be needed.

To prepare for the test the handbook includes information about what to expect together with practice questions and revision material.

Migration is a 'hot topic' in the UK. Successive governments continue to make adjustments to the visa categories and process that lead to settlement in the UK. Applicants are expected to comply with the rules in force when they make an application. These may be different from when the applicant first entered the country.

You can keep up to date with changes on the UK Visas and Immigration website or by asking your immigration advisor.

Because the UK settlement and visa rules are constantly changing we recommend that individuals take the Life in the UK Test as soon as possible. The Life in the UK Test pass certificate does not expire. You will not be asked to pass the Life in the UK Test more than once.

How to use this handbook

At the heart of this handbook is the section called 'Test Study Materials'. This section reproduces the official study material published in the UK government publication *'Life in the United Kingdom: A Guide for New Residents, Third edition'*. This material is also known as the 'Official Study Materials' or 'Published Study Materials'. Questions in the Life in the UK test are all based on these chapters. According to the Home Office candidates will only be tested on the 'published study materials' and not on the latest laws or regulations. The Home Office also removes questions if they have become out of date.

The Test Study Materials section is made up of five chapters reproduced from the official government publication:

Chapter 1: The values and principles of the UK
Chapter 2: What is the UK
Chapter 3: A long and illustrious history
Chapter 4: A modern thriving society
Chapter 5: The UK government, the law and your role

There are four different types of questions in the test. However, the actual questions in the test are a closely guarded secret. Revision time is best spent learning and understanding the 'Test Study Material'. It is not a good idea to try and memorize the answers to questions in this or other guides.

To help you revise this handbook includes lots of revision material after the Test Study materials' section. Inside you will find:

- A selection of 'Statements that are True' to help revision
- A full practice test
- A glossary with a list of essential words and phrases
- A comprehensive list of all people mentioned in the study material
- A list of the conflicts mentioned in the study material
- A list of all the battles mentioned in the study material
- A list of the annual calendar events from the study material; and
- A historic timeline for the UK showing key events you may be tested on

About the Life in the UK Test

UK immigration rules mean that anyone applying for Indefinite Leave to Remain (permanent settlement) or British Citizenship has to demonstrate 'Knowledge of language and of life in the United Kingdom' (KOLL). There are few exemptions.

The Life in the UK Test' was introduced in November 2005 as a way that British Citizens could demonstrate that the KOLL requirement had been met. This requirement was then extended to include those applying for Indefinite Leave to Remain.

Most people will have to pass the Life in the UK Test before they are able to apply for Indefinite Leave to Remain or British Citizenship. Since 28 October 2013 those seeking Indefinite Leave to Remain or British Citizenship are required to have a speaking and listening qualification in English at B1 CEFR (or higher, or an equivalent level qualification), as well as passing the Life in the UK Test.

Skilled and highly skilled migrants must now pass the Life in the UK Test if they want to demonstrate that they have met the knowledge of language and life (KOLL) requirement for settlement in the UK.

Key facts about the test
- The test contains 24 multiple choice questions in English
- The questions are based on the text of *Life in the United Kingdom: A Guide for New Residents*, 3rd Edition ISBN 9780113413409 (reproduced in full in this book).
- Questions are chosen at random by computer
- Applicants take the test using a computer provided by the test centre
- Applicants can listen to the questions using headphones provided by the test centre
- Applicants are given 45 minutes to complete the test
- The pass mark is 75% (18 questions correct out of 24)
- Each attempt to pass the test currently costs £50.00
- The test is conducted at around 60 Life in the UK Test Centres across the UK
- The current pass rate for the test is 70%
- You don't have to take the test if you are under the age of 18 or over 65
- Some people with physical or mental health conditions are also exempt.

When to take the test?
Take the test before you apply for naturalisation as a British citizen or for indefinite leave to remain.

How to book a test?
Since 2011 the tests have had to be booked online. You will need your own email address to book a test. Details of the 60 or so test centres in the UK can be found on the life in the UK website www.lifeintheuktest.gov.uk

Candidates now have to register, book and pay for their test online.

To do this you need to: Register for a Life in the UK account; Choose a test session; and Pay for your test

When you register for a Life in the UK account it is important that your details are correct as otherwise this could delay things later. The name printed on the certificate when you pass is the same as the name you enter when you register for a Life in the UK account.

There is a minimum waiting period of 7 days between making your booking and being able to take the test. (So if you fail a test you have to wait at least 7 days before taking it again). No refund is given if the test is cancelled less than 7 days before the test.

When you book you will be asked:

- Your name
- Date of birth
- Nationality
- Country of birth
- Town of birth;
- ID (identification that you are bringing to the test) – Passport, Photo driving licence, Approved travel doc, Home office travel doc, UK residence doc, Home office identity card

- You will be asked to confirm you have read *The Life in the United Kingdom: A Guide for New Residents, 3rd Edition*? Answer = 'Yes'.

- Why are you taking the test? Answer = 'Citizenship' or 'Settlement'

You will also be told what documents to bring with you and how to pay.

Documents to take with you to the test
The test supervisor requires proof of your identity. You will need to show the identity document that you said you would use when you booked the test.

Acceptable documents are: a passport from your country of origin (which may be out of date); A UK photocard driving licence (full or provisional); Home Office UK travel documents; a European Union Identity Card; an Immigration Status document; or A Biometric Residence Permit.

The test centre also needs the postcode from your address.

Make sure that you bring a gas, electric bill or water bill; a bank statement or credit card statement (a printed copy of a bank statement is acceptable however it must have been stamped and signed by the issuing branch); UK photocard driving licence or a letter from the Home Office with your name and address on it.

Taking the test
On arrival at your test centre, the test supervisor will confirm the things you entered when you booked the test.

- your full name
- date of birth
- nationality, country and place of birth
- postcode
- Home Office reference (if you have one)
- Your purpose for taking the test (for residence or for citizenship).
- Your photographic ID and proof of address will be checked.

You are expected to be able to answer the questions about the information on the identity documents, address, and reasons for taking the test, *without referring to the documents*. The Home Office state: "If you cannot do this correctly you will not be able to take the test and will not get a refund." There are many examples quoted online where people have been refused permission to take the test because of this. People have also been refused where the registered candidate's details don't match the ID and supporting documents exactly.

The other time that you might have problems being allowed to take the test is if you arrive late. The Home Office state: "We will send you an email to tell you what time to arrive at the test centre. If you do not arrive at the correct time, we may cancel your test and you will not get a refund."

Audio
You should request AUDIO and HEADPHONES during the arrival registration process if you want to be able to listen to the questions.

The audio should have been booked as a special requirement at the time you booked the test but most centres are flexible if you forgot to do this.

All of the 'getting ready' to take the test may take quite some time and feel very slow. Test centres vary considerably in terms of how efficiently they set you up.

You will be logged on to a computer and will have time to complete a practice test on your computer before you begin the Life in the UK Test. The test supervisor will tell you when to begin your test.

Once you start the test you have 45 minutes to complete it. There are 24 multiple choice questions. You have to get 18 correct to pass (75%). Most candidates complete the test within 30 minutes.

Test candidates are advised to expect to be at the test centre up to 2 hours in total.

Types of questions

The provider of the Life in the UK Test maintains a bank of a minimum of 300 approved questions. Each question in the question bank is expected to remain active for a maximum of 3 years. However, no question is exposed for more than 6 consecutive months.

The provider refreshes the question bank at least every 3 years. The test bank contains the following minimum number of tests for each region: England 20, Scotland 10, Wales 10 and Northern Ireland 10.

Where there is out of date content or the government requests withdrawal of specific questions there is a process to ensure this happens.

The performance of individual questions is analysed although none of the analysis has been made public.

The test itself contains four different types of question.

The 'official' example questions are reproduced below:

Question type 1
Select one correct answer from four options.

Example
Who is the patron saint of Scotland?
• St Andrew
• St George
• St David
• St Patrick

(*Answer = St Andrew*)

Question type 2
Decide whether a statement is true or false.

Example
Is the statement below TRUE or FALSE?

You have to be at least 21 years old before you can serve on a jury.

(*Answer = False*)

Question type 3
Select two correct answers from four options. [You have to pick two answers]

What is the name of the TWO houses that make up the UK Parliament?

• House of the People
• House of Commons
• House of Lords
• House of Government

(*Answer = House of Commons; and House of Lords*)

Question type 4
Select the correct statement from a choice of two statements.

Example
Which of these statements is correct?

• Nelson was a famous British military leader who died at the Battle of Trafalgar.
• Nelson was a famous British military leader who died at the Battle of Waterloo.

(*Answer = the first statement; Nelson died at Trafalgar*)

After the tests

At the end of the test, you will be issued with a Results Notification Letter. This will inform you if you have been successful or not.

If you fail

The Results Notification letter for those who fail the test will include text along the lines below:

"I regret to inform you, following your test today of knowledge of life in the United Kingdom, that you have not reached the level required for the purposes of obtaining indefinite leave to remain under the immigration rules or for naturalisation as a British Citizen under section 6 of the British Nationality Act 1981. You will be able to take the test again but we suggest some further study of the areas identified below before you do so. You should also check that you have enough valid leave to remain in the UK to enable you to take the test again. You should contact the Immigration Enquiry Bureau on 0870 6067766 if you have any enquiries about your leave to remain.

- The Black Death
- The Glorious Revolution
- The Welfare State
- Football
- The monarchy
- The cabinet
- The Commonwealth
- The judiciary
- Driving
- Becoming a good neighbour

Don't give up. Study some more and have another go.

You are allowed to take the test as many times as you want. Although you are not told the number of questions that you got right the list of sections where you answered incorrectly should enable you to work out how close you came.

If you pass
Successful candidates will receive a Pass Notification Letter signed and stamped by a Test Supervisor.

It is your responsibility to make sure that:
• you receive the correct result notification letter;
• you keep your result notification letter safe.

Your Results Notification Letter is an important document. Keep it safe as no replacement will be issued if you lose or damage it.

Although all test results are automatically sent to UK Visas and Immigration you still need to show your Results Notification Letter when applying for Indefinite Leave to Remain or British Citizenship.

The London Eye

Test Study Materials

The five chapters that follow contain all the material on which the questions in the Life in the UK Test are based.

- The values and principles of the UK

- What is the UK?

- A long and illustrious history

- A modern thriving society

- The UK Government, the law and your role

The chapters have been reproduced in full from the Home Office publication *'Life in the United Kingdom: A Guide for New Residents, 3rd edition.'*

The Union Jack

The values and principles of the UK

This section covers the responsibilities and privileges of being a British citizen or permanent resident of the UK

Britain is a fantastic place to live: a modern, thriving society with a long and illustrious history. Our people have been at the heart of the world's political, scientific, industrial and cultural development. We are proud of our record of welcoming new migrants who will add to the diversity and dynamism of our national life.

Applying to become a permanent resident or citizen of the UK is an important decision and commitment. You will be agreeing to accept the responsibilities which go with permanent residence and to respect the laws, values and traditions of the UK. Good citizens are an asset to the UK. We welcome those seeking to make a positive contribution to our society.

Passing the Life in the UK test is part of demonstrating that you are ready to become a permanent migrant to the UK. This handbook is designed to support you in your preparation. It will help you to integrate into society and play a full role in your local community. It will also help ensure that you have a broad general knowledge of the culture, laws and history of the UK.

The values and principles of the UK
British society is founded on fundamental values and principles which all those living in the UK should respect and support. These values are reflected in the responsibilities, rights and privileges of being a British citizen or permanent resident of the UK. They are based on history and traditions and are protected by law, customs and expectations.

There is no place in British society for extremism or intolerance.

The fundamental principles of British life include:
• Democracy
• The rule of law
• Individual liberty
• Tolerance of those with different faiths and beliefs
• Participation in community life

As part of the citizenship ceremony new citizens pledge to uphold these values.

The new citizens pledge is:

'I will give my loyalty to the United Kingdom and respect its rights and freedoms. I will uphold its democratic values. I will observe its laws faithfully and fulfil my duties as a British citizen.'

Following from the fundamental principles are 'responsibilities and freedoms' which are shared by all those living in the UK and which we expect all residents to respect.

If you wish to be a permanent resident of the UK, you should
- Respect and obey the law
- Respect the rights of others including their right to their own opinions
- Treat others with fairness
- Look after yourself and your family
- Look after the area in which you live and the environment,

In return, the UK offers:

- Freedom of belief and religion
- Freedom of speech
- Freedom from unfair discrimination
- A right to a fair trial
- A right to join in the election of a government

Becoming a permanent resident
From October 2013, new requirements came into force for those applying to become a permanent resident or citizen of the UK. From that date, for settlement or permanent residence, you will need to:

- Pass the Life in the UK Test

And

- Produce acceptable evidence of speaking and listening skills in English at B1 of the Common European Framework of Reference. This is equivalent to ESOL Entry Level 3.

The requirements for citizenship applications may also change in the future. Further details will be published on the UK Border Agency website and you should check the information on that website for current requirements before applying for settlement or citizenship.

A UK citizenship ceremony

Once you have passed one of these tests, you can make an application for permanent residence or British citizenship. The form that you have to complete and the evidence that you need to provide will depend on your personal circumstances. There is a fee for submitting an application, which is different for the various types of application. All of the forms and a list of fees can be found on UK Visas and Immigration website, www.gov.uk/government/organisations/uk-visas-and-immigration

Taking the Life in the UK test

This handbook [*The Life in the United Kingdom: A Guide for New Residents, 3rd edition* referred to now as 'The Study Material'] will prepare you for taking the Life in the UK test. The test itself consists of 24 questions about important aspects of life in the UK. Questions are based on ALL parts of the handbook [The Study Material]. The 24 questions will be different for each person taking the test at that test session.

The life in the UK test is usually taken in English, although special arrangements can be made if you wish to take it in Welsh or Scottish Gaelic.

You can only take the test at a registered and approved Life in the UK test centre. There are about 60 test centres around the UK. You can only book your test online, at *www.lifeintheuktest.gov.uk*. You should not take your test at any other establishment as the UK Visas and Immigration department will only accept certificates from registered centres. If you live on the Isle of Man or in the Channel Islands, there are different arrangements for taking the test.

When booking your test read the instructions carefully. Make sure you enter your details correctly. You will need to take some identification and proof of address with you to the test. If you don't take these, you will not be able to take the test.

How to use this handbook *[the guidance in the study material]*
Everything you will need to know to pass the Life in the UK test is included in this handbook. The questions will be based on the whole book, including this introduction, so make sure you study the entire book thoroughly.

The handbook has been written to ensure that anyone who can read English at ESOL Entry Level 3 or above should have no difficulty with the language.

The glossary at the back of the handbook contains some key words and phrases, which you might find helpful.

The 'Check that you understand boxes' are for guidance. They will help you to identify particular things that you should understand. Just knowing the things highlighted in these boxes will not be enough to pass the test. You need to make sure that you understand everything in the book, so please read the information carefully.

Where to find more information
You can find out more information from the following places:

The UK Visas and Immigration website (www.gov.uk/government/organisations/uk-visas-and-immigration) for more information about the application process and the forms you will need to complete.

The Life in the UK test website (www.lifeintheuktest.gov.uk) for more information about the test and how to book a place to take one.

Gov.uk (www.gov.uk) for information about ESOL courses and how to find one in your area.

Check that you understand
• *The origins of the values underlying British Society*
• *The fundamental principles of British life*
• *The responsibilities and freedoms which come with permanent residence*
• *The process of becoming a permanent resident or citizen*

What is the UK?

The UK is made up of England, Scotland, Wales and Northern Ireland. The rest of Ireland is an independent country.

The official name of the country is the United Kingdom of Great Britain and Northern Ireland. 'Great Britain' refers only to England, Scotland and Wales, not to Northern Ireland.

The words 'Britain', 'British Isles' or 'British', however, are used in this book to refer to everyone in the UK.

There are several islands which are closely linked with the UK but are not part of it: the Channel Islands and the Isle of Man. These have their own governments and are called 'Crown dependencies'.

There are also several British overseas territories in other parts of the world, such as St Helena and the Falkland Islands. They are also linked to the UK but are not part of it.

The UK is governed by the parliament sitting in Westminster. Scotland, Wales and Northern Ireland also have parliaments or assemblies of their own, with devolved powers in defined areas.

Check that you understand

• *The different countries that make up the UK*

Sutton Hoo helmet

A long and illustrious history

Chapter contents

EARLY BRITAIN

The first people to live in Britain were hunter gathers, in what we call the Stone Age. For much of the Stone Age, Britain was connected to the continent by a land bridge. People came and went, following the herds of deer and horses which they hunted. Britain only became permanently separated from the continent by the Channel about 10,000 years ago.

The first farmers arrived in Britain 6,000 years ago. The ancestors of these first farmers probably came from south-east Europe. These people built houses, tombs and monuments on the land.

One of these monuments, Stonehenge, still stands in what is now the English county of Wiltshire. Stonehenge was probably a special gathering place for seasonal ceremonies. Other Stone Ages sites have also survived. Skara Brae on Orkney, off the north coast of Scotland, is the best preserved prehistoric village in northern Europe, and has helped archaeologists to understand more about how people lived near the end of the Stone Age.

Around 4000 years ago people learned to make bronze. We call this period the Bronze Age. People lived in roundhouses and buried their dead in tombs called round barrows. The people of the Bronze Age were accomplished metalworkers who made many beautiful objects in bronze and gold, including tools, ornaments and weapons.

Stonehenge

The Bronze Age was followed by the Iron Age, when people learned how to make weapons and tools out of iron. People still lived in roundhouses, grouped together into larger settlements, and sometimes defended sites called hill forts. A very impressive hill fort can still be seen today at Maiden castle, in the English county of Dorset. Most people were farmers, craft workers or warriors.

The language they spoke was part of the Celtic language family. Similar languages are still spoken today in some parts of Wales, Scotland and Ireland. The people of the Iron Age had a sophisticated culture and economy. They made the first coins to be minted in Britain, some inscribed with the names of Iron Age kings. This marks the beginnings of British history.

The Romans

Julius Caesar led a Roman invasion of Britain in 55 BC. This was unsuccessful and for nearly 100 years Britain remained separate from the Roman Empire. In AD 43 Emperor Claudius led the Roman army in a new invasion. This time, there was resistance from some of the British tribes but the Romans were successful in occupying almost all of Britain. One of the tribal leaders who fought against the Romans was Boudicca,

Boudicca

the queen of the Iceni in what is now eastern England. She is still remembered today and there is a statue of her on Westminster Bridge in London, near the Houses of Parliament.

Areas of what is now Scotland were never conquered by the Romans, and the Emperor Hadrian built a wall in the north of England to keep out the Picts (ancestors of the Scottish people). Included in the wall were a number of forts.

Vindolanda Roman fort today

Parts of Hadrian's Wall, including the forts of Housteads and Vindolanda, can still be seen. It is a popular area for walkers and is a UNESCO (United National Educational, Scientific and Cultural Organisation) World Heritage Site.

The Romans remained in Britain for 400 years. They built roads and public buildings, created a structure of law, and introduced new plants and animals. It was during the 3rd and 4th centuries AD that the first Christian communities began to appear in Britain.

The Anglo-Saxons

The Roman army left Britain in AD 410 to defend other parts of the Roman Empire and never returned. Britain was again invaded by tribes

Sutton Hoo helmet.and sword

from northern Europe: the Jutes, the Angles and the Saxons. The languages they spoke are the basis of modern day English. Battles were fought against these invaders buy, by about AD 600 Anglo-Saxon kingdoms were established in Britain. These kingdoms were mainly in what is now England. The burial place of one of the kings was at Sutton Hoo in modern Suffolk. This king was buried with treasure and armour, all placed in a ship which was then covered by a mound of earth.

Parts of the west of Britain, including much of what is now Wales, and Scotland, remained free of Anglo-Saxon rule.

The Anglo-Saxons were not Christians when they first came to Britain but during this period, missionaries came to Britain to preach about Christianity. Missionaries from Ireland spread the religion in the north. The most famous of these were St Patrick, who would become the patron saint of Ireland, and St Columbia, who founded a monastery on the island of Iona, off the coast of what is now Scotland. St Augustine led missionaries from Rome, who spread Christianity in the south. St Augustine became the first Archbishop of Canterbury.

The Vikings

The Vikings came from Denmark and Norway. They first visited Britain in AD 789 to raid coastal towns and take away goods and slaves. Then, they began to stay and form their own communities in the east of England and Scotland. The Anglo-Saxon

King Alfred the Great

25

A Viking long ship

kingdoms in England united under King Alfred the Great, who defeated the Vikings. Many of the Viking invaders stayed in Britain – especially in the east and north of England, in an area known as the Danelaw (many place names there, such as Grimsby and Scunthorpe, come from the Viking languages).

The Viking settlers mixed with local communities and some converted to Christianity. Anglo-Saxon kings continued to rule what is now England, except for a short period when there were Danish kings. The first of these was Cnut, also called Canute.

In the north, the threat of attack by Vikings had encouraged the people to unite under one king, Kenneth MacAlpin. The term Scotland began to be used to describe that country.

William the Conqueror

The Norman Conquest

In 1066, an invasion led by William, the Duke of Normandy (in what is now northern France), defeated Harold, the Saxon king of England, at the Battle of Hastings. Harold was killed in the battle. William became king of England and is known as William the Conqueror. The battle is commemorated in a great piece of embroidery, known as the Bayeux Tapestry, which can still be seen in France today.

The Norman Conquest was the last successful foreign invasion of England and led

Part of the Bayeux Tapestry

to many changes in government and social structures in England. Norman French, the language of the new ruling class, influenced the development of the English language as we know it today. Initially the Normans also conquered Wales, but the Welsh gradually won the territory back.

The Scots and the Normans fought on the border between England and Scotland; the Normans took over some land on the border but did not invade Scotland.

William sent people all over England to draw up lists of all the towns and villages. The people who lived there, who owned the land and what animals they owned were also listed. This was called the Domesday Book. It still exists today and gives a picture of the society in England just after the Norman Conquest.

Domesday book extract

Check that you understand
- *The history of the UK before the Romans*
- *The impact of the Romans on British Society*
- *The different groups that invaded after the Romans*
- *The importance of the Norman invasion of 1066*

THE MIDDLE AGES

War at home and abroad
The period after the Norman Conquest up until about 1485 is called the Middle Ages (or the medieval period). It was a time of almost constant war.

The English knights fought with the Welsh, Scottish and Irish noblemen for control of their lands. In Wales, the English were able to establish their rule. In 1284 King Edward I of England introduced the Statute of Rhuddlan, which annexed Wales to the Crown of England. Huge castles, including Conwy and Caernarvon, were built to maintain this power. By the middle of the 15th century

Caernarvon castle today

Statue of Robert the Bruce

the last Welsh rebellions had been defeated. English laws and the English language were introduced.

In Scotland, the English kings were less successful. In 1314 the Scottish, led by Robert the Bruce, defeated the English at the Battle of Bannockburn, and Scotland remained unconquered by the English.

At the beginning of the Middle Ages, Ireland was an independent country. The English first went to Ireland as troops to help the Irish king and remained to build their own settlements. By 1200, the English ruled an area of Ireland known as the Pale, around Dublin. Some of the important lords in other parts of Ireland accepted the authority of the English king.

King Henry V at Agincourt

During the Middle Ages, the English kings also fought a number of wars abroad. Many knights took part in the Crusades, in which European Christians fought for control of the Holy Land.

English kings also fought a long war with France, called the Hundred Years War (even though it actually lasted 116 years).

One of the most famous battles of the Hundred Years War was the Battle of Agincourt in 1415, where King Henry V's vastly outnumbered English army defeated the French. The English left France in the 1450s.

The Black Death

The Normans used a system of land ownership known as feudalism. The king gave land to his lords in return for help in war. Landowners had to send certain numbers of men to serve in the army.

Some peasants had their own land but most were serfs. They had a small area of their lord's land where they could grow food. In return, they had to work for their lord and could not move away. The same system developed in southern Scotland. In the north of Scotland and Ireland, land was owned by members of the 'clans' (prominent families).

In 1348, a disease, probably a form of plague, came to Britain. This was known as the Black Death. One third of the population of England died and a similar proportion in Scotland and Wales. This was one of the disasters ever to strike Britain. Following the Black Death, the smaller population meant there was less need to grow cereal crops. There were labour shortages and peasants began to demand higher wages. New social classes appeared, including the owners of large areas of land (later called the gentry), and people left the countryside to live in towns. In the towns, growing wealth led to the development of a strong middle class.

A Black Death plague doctor

In Ireland, the Black Death killed many in the Pale and, for a time, the area controlled by the English became smaller.

Legal and political changes

In the Middle Ages, Parliament began to develop into the institution it is today. Its origins can be traced to the king's council of advisers, which included important noblemen and the leaders of the Church.

Magna Carta

There were few formal limits to the king's power until 1215. In that year, King John was forced by his noblemen to agree to a number of demands. The result was a charter of rights called the Magna Carta (which means Great Charter). The Magna Carta established the idea that even the king was subject to the law. It protected the rights of the nobility and restricted the king's power to collect taxes or to make or change laws. In future, the king would need to involve his noblemen in decisions.

In England, parliaments were called for the king to consult his nobles, particularly when the king needed to raise money. The numbers attending Parliament increased and two separate parts, known as Houses, were established. The nobility, great landowners and bishops sat in the House of Lords. Knights, who were usually smaller

The Prioress and the Knight from the Canterbury tales of 1485

landowners and wealthy people from towns and cities, were elected to sit in the House of Commons. Only a small part of the population was able to join in electing the members of the Commons.

A similar Parliament developed in Scotland. It had three Houses, called Estates: the lords, the commons and the clergy.

This was also a time of development in the legal system. The principle that judges are independent of the government began to be established. In England, judges developed 'common law' by a process of precedence (that is, following previous decisions). In Scotland, the legal system developed slightly differently and laws were 'codified' (that is written down).

A distinct identity

The Middle Ages saw the development of a national culture and identity. After the Norman Conquest, the king and his noblemen had spoken Norman French and the peasants had continued to speak Anglo-Saxon. Gradually these two languages combined to become one English language. Some words in modern English – for example, 'park' and 'beauty' – are based on Norman French words. Others – for example, 'apple', 'cow' and 'summer' – are based on Anglo-Saxon words. In modern English there are often two words with very similar meanings, one from French and one from Anglo-Saxon. 'Demand' (French) and 'ask' (Anglo-Saxon) are examples. By 1400, in England, official documents were being written in English, and English had become the preferred language in the royal court and Parliament.

Geoffrey Chaucer

In the years leading up to 1400, Geoffrey Chaucer wrote a series of poems in English about a group of people going to Canterbury on a pilgrimage. The people decided to tell each other stories on the journey, and the poems describe the travelers and some of the stories they told. This collection of poems is called *The Canterbury Tales*. It was one of the first books to be printed by William

Caxton, the first person in England to print books using a printing press. Many of the stories are still popular. Some have been made into plays and television programmes.

York Minster stained glass

In Scotland, many people continued to speak Gaelic and the Scots language also developed. A number of poets began to write in the Scots language. One example is John Barbour, who wrote The Bruce about the Battle of Bannockburn.

The Middle Ages also saw a change in the type of buildings in Britain. Castles were built in many places in Britain and Ireland, partly for defence. Today many are in ruins, although some, such as Windsor and Edinburgh are still in use. Great cathedrals – for example, Lincoln Cathedral – were also built, and many of these are still used for worship. Several of the cathedrals had windows of stained glass, telling stories about the Bible and Christian saints. The glass in York Minster is a famous example.

During the period, England was an important trading nation. English wool became a very important export. People came to England from abroad to trade and also to work. Many had special skills, such as weavers from France, engineers from Germany, glass manufacturers from Italy and canal builders from Holland.

Red rose of Lancaster and white rose of York

The Wars of the Roses

In 1455, a civil war was begun to decide who should be king of England. It was fought between supporters of two families: the House of Lancaster and the House of York. This war was called the Wars of the Roses, because the symbol of Lancaster was a red rose and the symbol of York was a white rose. The war ended with the Battle of Bosworth Field in 1485. King Richard III of the House of York was killed in the battle and Henry Tudor, the leader of the House of Lancaster, became

Richard III died at the Battle of Bosworth Field

31

King Henry VII. Henry then married King Richard's niece, Elizabeth of York, and united the two families. Henry was the first king of the House of Tudor. The symbol of the House of Tudor was a red rose with a white rose inside it as a sign that the Houses of York and Lancaster were now allies.

Check that you understand
- *The wars that took place in the Middle Ages*
- *How Parliament began to develop*
- *The way that land ownership worked*
- *The effects of the Black Death*
- *The development of English language and culture*
- *The Wars of the Roses and the founding of the House of Tudor*

Henry VII

Henry VIII

THE TUDORS AND STUARTS

Religious conflicts

After his victory in the Wars of the Roses, Henry VII wanted to make sure that England remained peaceful and that his position as king was secure. He deliberately strengthened the central administration of England and reduced the power of the nobles. He was thrifty and built up the monarchy's financial reserves. When he died, his son Henry VIII continued the policy of centralizing power.

Henry VIII was most famous for breaking away from the Church of Rome and marrying six times.

To divorce his first wife, Henry needed the approval of the Pope. When the Pope refused, Henry established the Church of England. In this new Church, the king, not the Pope, would have the power to appoint bishops and order how people should worship.

At the same time the Reformation was happening across Europe. This was a movement against the authority of the Pope and the ideas and practices of the Roman Catholic Church. The Protestants formed their own churches. They read the Bible in their own

The six wives of Henry VIII

Catherine of Aragon – Catherine was a Spanish princess. She and Henry had a number of children but only one, Mary, survived. When Catherine was too old to give him another child, Henry decided to divorce her, hoping that another wife could give him a son to be his heir.

Anne Boleyn – Anne Boleyn was English. She and Henry had one daughter, Elizabeth. Anne was unpopular in the country and was accused of taking lovers. She was executed at the Tower of London.

Jane Seymour – Henry married Jane after Anne's execution. She gave Henry the son he wanted, Edward, but she died shortly after his birth.

Anne of Cleves – Anne was a German princess. Henry married her for political reasons but divorced her soon after.

Catherine Howard – Catherine was cousin of Anne Boleyn. She was also accused of taking lovers and executed.

Catherine Parr – Catherine was a widow who married Henry late in his life. She survived him and married again but died soon after.

languages instead of in Latin; they did not pray to saints or at shrines; and they believed that a person's own relationship with God was more important than submitting to the authority of the Church. Protestant ideas gradually gained strength in England, Wales and Scotland during the 16th century.

In Ireland, however, attempts by the English to impose Protestantism (alongside efforts to introduce the English system of laws about the inheritance of land) led to rebellion from the Irish chieftains and much brutal fighting followed.

During the reign of Henry VIII, Wales became formally united with England by the Act for the Government of Wales. The Welsh sent representatives to the House of Commons and the Welsh legal system was reformed.

Henry VIII was succeeded by his son Edward VI, who was strongly Protestant. During his reign, the Book of Common Prayer was written to be used in the Church of England. A version of this book is still used in some churches today. Edward died at the age of 15 after ruling for just over 6 years, and his half-sister Mary became queen. Mary was a devout Catholic and persecuted

Edward VI

Mary I (Bloody Mary)

Protestants (for this reason she became known as 'Bloody Mary'). Mary also died after a short reign and the next monarch was her half-sister, Elizabeth, the daughter of Henry VIII and Anne Boleyn.

Queen Elizabeth

Queen Elizabeth I was a Protestant. She re-established the Church of England as the official church and there were laws about the type of religious services and the prayers which could be said, but Elizabeth did not ask about people's real beliefs.

She succeeded in finding a balance between the views of Catholics and the more extreme Protestants. In this way she avoided any serious religious conflict within England. Elizabeth became one of the most popular monarchs in English history, particularly after 1588, when the English defeated the Spanish Armada (a large fleet of ships), which had been sent by Spain to conquer England and restore Catholicism.

Queen Elizabeth I

The reformation in Scotland and Mary, Queen of Scots

Scotland had also been strongly influenced by Protestant ideas. In 1560, the predominantly Protestant Scottish Parliament abolished the authority of the Pope in Scotland and Roman Catholic religious services became illegal. A Protestant Church of Scotland with an elected leadership was established but, unlike in England, this was not a state Church.

The queen of Scotland, Mary Stuart (often now called 'Mary' Queen of Scots') was a Catholic. She was only a week old when her father died and she became queen. Much of her childhood was spent in France.

When she returned to Scotland, she was the centre of a power struggle between different groups.

Mary Stuart

When her husband was murdered, Mary was suspected of involvement and fled to England. She gave her throne to her protestant son, James VI of Scotland.

Execution of Mary Stuart

Mary was Elizabeth I's cousin and hoped that Elizabeth might help her, but Elizabeth suspected Mary of wanting to take over the English throne, and kept her a prisoner for 20 years. Mary was eventually executed, accused of plotting against Elizabeth I

Exploration, poetry and drama

The Elizabethan period in England was a time of growing patriotism: a feeling of pride in being English. English explorers sought new trade routes and tried to expand British trade into the Spanish colonies in the Americas.

Sir Francis Drake, one of the commanders in the defeat of the Spanish Armada, was one of the founders of England's naval tradition. His ship, the Golden Hind, was one of the first to sail right around ('circumnavigate') the world. In Elizabeth I's time, English settlers first began to colonise the eastern coast of America. This colonization, particularly by people who disagreed with the religious views of the next two kings, greatly increased in the next century.

Sir Francis Drake

The Elizabethan period is also remembered for the richness of its poetry and drama, especially the plays and poems of William Shakespeare.

William Shakespeare (1564-1616)

Shakespeare is widely regarded as the greatest writer in the English language

Shakespeare was born in Stratford-upon-Avon, England. He was a playwright and wrote many poems and plays. His most famous plays include *A Midsummer Night's Dream*, *Hamlet*, *Macbeth* and *Romeo and Juliet*. He also dramatized significant events from the past, but he did not focus solely on kings and queens. He was one of the first to portray ordinary Englishmen and women. Shakespeare had a great influence on the English language and invented many words that are still common today. Lines from his plays and poems which are still quoted include:

- 'Once more unto the breach' (*Henry V*)

- 'To be or not to be' (*Hamlet*)

- 'A rose by any other name' (*Romeo and Juliet*)

- 'All the world's a stage (*As you like it*)

- The darling buds of May (Sonnet 18 – *Shall I Compare Thee To A Summer's Day*).

Many people regard Shakespeare as the greatest playwright of all time. His plays and poems are still performed and studied in Britain and other countries today. The Globe Theater in London is a modern copy of the theatres in which his plays were performed.

James VI and I

Elizabeth I never married and so had no children on her own to inherit her throne. When she died in 1603 her heir was her cousin James VI of Scotland.

He became King James I of England, Wales and Ireland but Scotland remained a separate country.

James IV and I

The King James Bible

One achievement of King James' reign was a new translation of the Bible into English. This translation is known as the 'King James Version' or the 'Authorised Version'. It was not the first English Bible but it is a version which continues to be used in many Protestant churches today.

Ireland

During this period, Ireland was an almost completely Catholic country. Henry VII and Henry VIII had extended English control outside 'the Pale' and established English authority over the whole of the country. Henry VIII took the title 'King of Ireland'. English laws were introduced and local leaders were expected to follow the instructions of the Lord Lieutenants in Dublin.

During the reigns of Elizabeth I and James I, many people in Ireland opposed rule by the Protestant government in England. There were a number of rebellions. The English government encouraged Scottish and English Protestants to settle in Ulster, the northern province of Ireland, taking over the land from Catholic landowners. These settlements were known as plantations. Many of the new settlers came from south-west Scotland and other land was given to companies based in London. James later organised similar plantations in several other parts of Ireland. This had serious long-term consequences for the history of England, Scotland and Ireland.

The rise of Parliament

Elizabeth I was very skilled at managing Parliament. During her reign she was successful in balancing her wishes and views against those of the House of Lords and those of the House of Commons, which was increasingly Protestant in its views

Charles I

James I and his son Charles I were less skilled politically. Both believed in the 'Divine Right of Kings': the idea that the king was directly appointed by God to rule. They thought that the king should be able to act without having to seek approval from Parliament.

When Charles I inherited the thrones of England, Wales and Ireland and Scotland, he tried to rule in line with this principle. When he could not get Parliament to agree with his religious and foreign policies, he tried to rule without Parliament at all. For 11 years, he found ways in which to raise money without Parliaments approval but eventually trouble in Scotland meant that he had to recall Parliament.

The beginning of the English Civil War

Charles I wanted the worship of the Church of England to include more ceremony and introduced a revised Prayer Book. He tried to impose this Prayer Book on the Presbyterian Church in Scotland and this led to serious unrest. A Scottish army was formed and Charles could not find the money he needed for his own army without the help of Parliament. In 1640, he recalled Parliament to ask it for funds.

Civil war muskets

Many in Parliament were Puritans, a group of Protestants who advocated strict and simple religious doctrine and worship. They did not agree with the king's religious views and disliked his reforms of the Church of England. Parliament refused to give the king the money he asked for, even after the Scottish army invaded England.

A roundhead soldier

Another rebellion began in Ireland because the Roman Catholics in Ireland were afraid of the growing power of the Puritans. Parliament took this opportunity to demand control of the English army – a change that would have transferred substantial power from the king to Parliament. In response, Charles I entered the House of Commons and tried to arrest five parliamentary leaders, but they had been warned and were not there. (No monarch has set foot in the Commons since.)

Civil war between the king and Parliament could not now be avoided and began in 1642. The country split into those who supported the king (the Cavaliers) and those who supported Parliament (the Roundheads)

Oliver Cromwell and the English republic

The king's army was defeated at the Battles of Marston Moor and Naseby. By 1646, it was clear that Parliament had won the war. Charles was held prisoner by the parliamentary army. He was still unwilling to reach any agreement with Parliament and in 1649 he was executed.

Oliver Cromwell

England declared itself a republic, called the Commonwealth. It no longer had a monarch. For a time, it was not totally clear how the country would be governed. For now, the army was in control. One of its generals, Oliver Cromwell, was sent to Ireland, where the revolt which had begun in 1641 still continued and where there was still a Royalist army. Cromwell was successful in establishing the authority of the English Parliament but did this with such violence that even today Cromwell remains a controversial figure in Ireland.

The Scots had not agreed to the execution of Charles I and declared his son Charles II to be king. He was crowned king of Scotland and led a Scottish army into England. Cromwell defeated this army at the Battles of Dunbar and Worcester. Charles II escaped from Worcester, famously hiding in an oak tree on one occasion, an eventually fled to Europe. Parliament now controlled Scotland as well as England and Wales.

The Battle of Worcester

After his campaign in Ireland and victory over Charles II at Worcester, Cromwell was recognised as the leader of the new republic. He was given the title of Lord Protector and ruled until his death in 1658. When Cromwell died, his son, Richard, became Lord Protector in his place but was not able to control the army or the government. Although Britain had been a republic for 11 years, without Oliver Cromwell there was no clear leader or system of government. Many people in the country wanted stability. People began to talk about the need for a king.

The Restoration

In May 1660, Parliament invited Charles II to come back from exile in the Netherlands. He was crowned King Charles II of England, Wales, Scotland

and Ireland. Charles II made it clear that he had 'no wish to go on his travels again'. He understood that he could not always do as he wished but would sometimes need to reach agreement with Parliament. Generally, Parliament supported his policies. The Church of England again became the established official Church. Both Roman Catholics and Puritans were kept out of power.

During Charles II's reign, in 1665, there was a major outbreak of plague in London. Thousands of people died, especially in poorer areas. The following year, a great fire destroyed much of the city, including many churches and St Paul's Cathedral. London was rebuilt with a new St Paul's, which was

Charles II

designed by famous architect, Sir Christopher Wren. Samuel Pepys wrote about these events in a diary which was later published and is still read today.

The Habeas Corpus Act became law in 1679. This was a very important piece of legislation which remains relevant today.

Habeas corpus is Latin for 'you must present the person to court'. The Act guaranteed that no one could be held prisoner unlawfully. Every prisoner has a right to a court hearing.

Charles II was interested in science. During his reign the Royal Society was formed to promote 'natural knowledge'. This is the oldest surviving scientific society in the world. Among its early members were Sir Edmund Halley, who successfully predicted the return of the comet now called Halley's Comet, and Sir Isaac Newton.

Halley's comet

Isaac Newton (1643-1727)

Born in Lincolnshire, eastern England, Isaac Newton
first became interested in science when he studied at
Cambridge University. He became an important figure
in the field. His most famous published work was
Philosophiae Naturalis Principia Mathematica
('Mathematical Principles of Natural Philosophy'),
which showed how gravity applied to the whole
universe. Newton also showed that white light is made
up of the colours of the rainbow. Many of his
discoveries are still important for modern science.

A Catholic King

Charles II had no legitimate children. He died in 1685 and his brother James,
who was a Roman Catholic, became King James II in England, Wales and Ireland

and King James VII of Scotland. James favoured Roman
Catholics and allowed them to be army officers, which
an Act of Parliament had forbidden. He did not seek to
reach agreements with Parliament and arrested some
of the bishops of the Church of England. People in
England worried that James wanted to make England a
Catholic country once more. However, his heirs were
his two daughters, who were both firmly Protestant, and
people thought that this meant that there would soon be a
Protestant monarch again. Then, James's wife had a son.
Suddenly, it seemed likely that the next monarch would
not be a Protestant after all.

James II

The Glorious Revolution

James II's elder daughter, Mary was married to her
cousin William of Orange, the Protestant ruler of the
Netherlands. In 1688, important Protestants in England
asked William to invade England and proclaim himself
king. When William reached England there was no
resistance. James fled to France and William took over
the throne, becoming William III in England, Wales
and Ireland and William II of Scotland. William ruled
jointly with Mary. This event was later called the

William III

'Glorious Revolution' because there was no fighting in England and because it guaranteed the power of Parliament, ending the threat of a monarch ruling on his or her own as he or she wished. James II wanted to regain the throne and invaded Ireland with the help of a French army.

William defeated James II at the Battle of the Boyne in Ireland in 1690, an event which is still celebrated by some in Northern Ireland today. William re-conquered Ireland and James fled back to France. Many restrictions were placed on the Roman Catholic Church in Ireland and Irish Catholics were unable to take part in the government.

The Battle of the Boyne

There was also support for James in Scotland. An attempt at an armed rebellion in support of James was quickly defeated at Killiecrankie. All Scottish clans were required formally to accept William as king by taking an oath.

The MacDonald's of Glencoe were late in taking the oath and were all killed. The memory of this massacre meant some Scots distrusted the new government.

Some continued to believe that James was the rightful king, particularly in Scotland. Some joined him in exile in France; others were secret supporters. James' supporters became known as Jacobites.

Check that you understand
- *How and why religion changed during this period*
- *The importance of poetry and drama in the Elizabethan period.*
- *About the involvement of Britain in Ireland*
- *The development of Parliament and the only period in history when England was a republic*
- *Why there was a restoration of the monarchy*
- *How the Glorious Revolution happened*

A GLOBAL POWER

Constitutional monarchy – the Bill of Rights

At the coronation of William and Mary, a Declaration of Rights was read. This confirmed that the king would no longer be able to raise taxes or administer justice without agreement from Parliament. The balance of power between the monarch and Parliament had now permanently changed.

The Bill of Rights, 1689, confirmed the rights of Parliament and the limits of the king's power. Parliament took control of who could be monarch and declared that the king or queen must be a Protestant. A new Parliament had to be elected at least every three years (later this became seven years and now it is five years).

Every year the monarch had to ask Parliament to renew funding for the army and the navy.

The Bill of Rights

These changes meant that, to be able to govern effectively, the monarch needed to have advisers, or ministers, who would be able to ensure a majority of votes in the House of Commons and the House of Lords.

There were two main groups in Parliament, known as the Whigs and the Tories. (The modern Conservative Party is still sometimes referred to as the Tories.) This was the beginning of party politics.

This was also an important time for the development of a free press (newspapers and other publications which are not controlled by the government). From 1695, newspapers were allowed to operate without a government licence. Increasing numbers of newspapers began to be published.

Whigs and Tories

The laws passed after the Glorious Revolution are the beginning of what is called 'constitutional monarchy'. The monarch remained very important but was no longer able to insist on particular policies or actions if Parliament did not agree. After William III, the ministers gradually became more important than the monarch but this was not a democracy in the modern sense. The number of people who had the right to vote for members of Parliament was still very small. Only men who owned property of a certain value were able to vote. No women at all had the vote. Some constituencies were controlled by a single wealthy family. These were called 'pocket boroughs'. Other constituencies had hardly any voters and were called 'rotten boroughs'.

A growing population
This was a time when many people left Britain and Ireland to settle in new colonies in America and elsewhere, but others came to live in Britain. The first Jews to come to Britain since the Middle Ages settled in London in 1656. Between 1680 and 1720   many refugees called Huguenots came from France. They were Protestant and had been persecuted for their religion. Many were educated and skilled and worked as scientists, in banking, or in weaving or other crafts.

The Act or Treaty of Union in Scotland
William and Mary's successor, Queen Anne, had no surviving children. This created uncertainty over the succession in England, Wales and Ireland and in Scotland.

The Act of Union, known as the Treaty of Union in Scotland, was therefore agreed in 1707, creating the Kingdom of Great Britain. Although Scotland was no longer an independent country, it kept its own legal and education systems and Presbyterian Church.

Queen Anne

The Prime Minister
When Queen Anne died in 1714, Parliament chose a German, George I, to be the next king, because he was Anne's nearest Protestant relative. An attempt by Scottish Jacobites to put James II's son on the throne instead was quickly defeated. George I did not speak very good English and this increased his need to rely on his ministers. The most important minister in Parliament became known as the Prime Minister. The first man to be called this was Sir Robert Walpole, who was Prime Minister from 1721 to 1742.

Sir Robert Walpole

The rebellion of the clans

In 1745 there was another attempt to put a Stuart king back on the throne in place of George I's so. Charles Edward Stuart (Bonnie Prince Charlie), the grandson of James II, landed in Scotland. He was supported by clansmen from the Scottish Highlands and raised an army.

Charles initially had some successes but was defeated by George II's army at the Battle of Culloden in 1746. Charles escaped back to Europe.

The clans lost a lot of their power and influence after Culloden. Chieftains became landlords if they had the favour of the English king, and clansmen became tenants who had to pay for the land they used.

A process began which became known as the 'Highland Clearances'. Many Scottish landlords destroyed individual small farms (known as 'crofts') to make space for large flocks of sheep and cattle. Evictions became very common in the early 19th century. Many Scottish people left for North America at this time.

The Battle of Culloden

Robert Burns (1759-96)

Known in Scotland as 'The Bard', Robert Burns was a Scottish poet. He wrote in the Scots language, English with some Scottish words, and standard English. He also revised a lot of traditional folk songs by changing or adding lyrics. Burns' best-known work is probably the song Auld Lang Syne, which is sung by people in the UK and other countries when they are celebrating the New Year or Hogmanay as it is called in Scotland).

The Enlightenment

During the 18th century, new ideas about politics, philosophy and science were developed. This is often called 'the Enlightenment'. Many of the great thinkers of the Enlightenment were Scottish. Adam Smith developed ideas about

economics which are still referred to today. David Hume's ideas about human nature continue to influence philosophers. Scientific discoveries, such as James Watt's work on steam power, helped the progress of the Industrial Revolution.

One of the most important principles of the Enlightenment was that everyone should have the right to their own political and religious beliefs and that the state should not try to dictate to them. This continues to be an important principle of the UK today.

Adam Smith

The Industrial Revolution

Before the 18th century, agriculture was the biggest source of employment in Britain. There were many collage industries, where people worked from home to produce goods such as cloth and lace.

The Industrial Revolution was the rapid development of industry in Britain in the 18th and 19th centuries. Britain was the first country to industrialise on a large scale. It happened because of the development of machinery and the use of steam power. Agriculture and the

Richard Arkwright (1732-92)

Born in 1732, Arkwright originally trained and worked as a barber. He was able to dye hair and make wigs. When wigs became less popular, he started to work in textiles. He improved the original carding machines. Carding is the process of preparing fibres for spinning into yarn and fabric. He also developed horse-driven spinning mills that used only one machine. This increased the efficiency of production. Later he used the steam engine to power machinery. Arkwright is particularly remembered for the efficient and profitable way that he ran his factories.

manufacturing of goods became mechanized. This made things more efficient and increased production. Coal and other raw materials were needed to power the new factories.

Many people moved from the countryside and started working in the mining and manufacturing industries.

The development of the Bessemer process for the mass production of steel led to the development of the shipbuilding industry and railways. Manufacturing jobs became the main source of employment in Britain.

Better transport links were needed to transport raw materials and manufactured goods. Canals were built to link the factories to towns and cities and to the ports, particularly in the new industrial areas in the middle and north of England.

Working conditions during the Industrial Revolution were very poor. There were no laws to protect employees, who were often forced to work long hours in dangerous situations. Children also worked and were treated in the same way as adults. Sometimes they were treated even more harshly.

This was also the time of increased colonization overseas. Captain James Cook mapped the coast of Australia and a few colonies were established there. Britain gained control over Canada, and the east India Company, originally set up to trade, gained control of large parts of India. Colonies began to be established in southern Africa.

Britain traded all over the world and began to import more goods. Sugar and tobacco came from North America and the West Indies; textiles, tea and spices came from India and the area that is today called Indonesia.

Trading and settlement overseas sometimes brought Britain into conflict with other countries, particularly France, which was expanding and trading in a similar way in many of the same areas of the world.

Sake Dean Mahomet (1759-1851)

Mahomet was born in 1759 and grew up in the Bengal region of India. He served in the Bengal army and came to Britain in 1782. He then moved to Ireland and eloped with and Irish girl called Jane Daly in 1786, returning to England at the turn of the century. In 1810 he opened the Hindoostane Coffee House in George Street, London. It was the first curry house to open in Britain. Mahomet and his wife also introduced 'shampooing', the Indian art of head massage, to Britain.

The slave trade

The commercial expansion and prosperity was sustained in part by the booming slave trade. While slavery was illegal within Britain itself, by the 18th century it was a fully established overseas industry, dominated by Britain and the American colonies.

Slaves came primarily from West Africa. Travelling on British ships in horrible conditions, they were taken to America and the Caribbean, where they were made to work on tobacco and sugar plantations. The living and working conditions for slaves were very bad. Many slaves tried to escape and others revolted against their owners in protest at their terrible treatment.

Slave trading

There were, however, people in Britain who opposed the slave trade. The first formal anti-slavery groups were set up by the Quakers in the late 1700s, and they petitioned Parliament to ban the practice.

William Wilberforce, an evangelical Christian and a member of Parliament, also played a part in changing the law. Along with other abolitionists (people who supported the abolition of slavery), he succeeded in turning public opinion against the slave trade.

William Wilberforce

In 1807, it became illegal to trade slaves in British ships or from British ports, and in 1833 the Emancipation Act abolished slavery throughout the British Empire. The Royal Navy stopped slave ships from other countries, freed the slaves, and punished the slave traders.

After 1833, 2 million Indian and Chinese workers were employed to replace the freed slaves. They worked on sugar plantations in the Caribbean, in mines in South Africa, on railways in East Africa and in the army in Kenya.

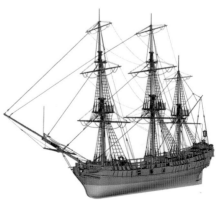

Model of a slave ship

The American War of Independence

By the 1760s, there were substantial British colonies in North America. The colonies were wealthy and largely in control of their own affairs. Many of the colonist families had originally gone to North America in order to have religious freedom. They were well educated and interested in ideas of liberty. The British government wanted to tax the colonies. The colonists saw this as an attack on their freedom and said there should be 'no taxation without representation' in the British Parliament.

British red coat

Parliament tried to compromise by repealing some of the taxes, but relationships between the British government and the colonies continued to worsen. Fighting broke out between the colonists and the British forces. In 1766, 13 American colonies declared their independence, stating that people had a right to establish their own governments.

The colonists eventually defeated the British army and Britain recognised the colonies independence in 1783.

War with France

During the 18th century, Britain fought a number of wars with France. In 1789, there was a revolution in France and the new French government soon declared war on Britain. Napoleon, who became Emperor of France, continued the war.

Britain's navy fought against combined French and Spanish fleets, winning the Battle of Trafalgar in 1805. Admiral Nelson was in charge of the British fleet at Trafalgar and was killed in the battle. Nelson's Column in Trafalgar square, London is a monument to him. His ship HMS Victory can be visited in Portsmouth.

The Battle of Trafalgar (21 Ocotber 1805) was a naval engagement fought by the British Royal Navy against the combined fleets of the French Navy and Spanish Navy

Admiral Nelson

In 1815, the French wars ended with the defeat of the Emperor Napoleon by the Duke of Wellington at the Battle of Waterloo. Wellington was known as the Iron Duke and later became Prime Minister.

The Duke of Wellington

The Union Flag

Although Ireland had the same monarch as England and Wales since Henry VIII, it had remained a separate country. In 1801, Ireland became unified with England, Scotland and Wales after the Act of Union of 1800. This created the United Kingdom of Great Britain and Ireland. One symbol of this union between England, Scotland, Wales and Ireland was a new version of the official flag, the Union Flag. This is often called the Union Jack. The flag combined crosses associated with England, Scotland and Ireland. It is still used today as the official flag of the UK.

The Union Jack

The Union Flag consists of three crosses:

1. The cross of St George, patron saint of England, is a red cross on a white background
2. The cross of St Andrew, patron saint of Scotland, is a diagonal white cross on a blue background.
3. The cross of St Patrick, patron saint of Ireland, is a diagonal red cross on a white ground.

There is also an official Welsh flag, which shows a Welsh dragon. The Welsh dragon does not appear on the Union Flag because, when the first Union Flag was created in 1606 from the flags of Scotland and England, the Principality of Wales was already united with England.

The crosses of England, Scotland and Ireland that make up the Union Jack

The Welsh flag

The Victorian Age

Queen Victoria

In 1837, Queen Victoria became queen of the UK at the age of 18. She reigned until 1901, almost 64 years. At the day of writing (2013) this is the longest reign of any British monarch (*note: record now held by Queen Elizabeth II*). Her reign is known as the Victorian Age. It was a time when Britain increased in power and influence abroad.

Within the UK, the middle classes became increasingly significant and a number of reformers led moves to improve conditions for the poor.

The British Empire

During the Victorian period, the British Empire grew to cover all of India, Australia and large parts of Africa. It became the largest empire the world has ever seen, with an estimated population of more than 400 million people.

Many people were encouraged to leave the UK to settle overseas. Between 1853 and 1913, as many as 13 million British citizens left the country. People continued to come to Britain from other parts of the world. For example, between 1870 and 1914, around 120,000 Russian and Polish Jews came to Britain to escape persecution. Many settled in London's East End and in Manchester and Leeds.

People from the Empire, including India and Africa, also came to Britain to live, work and study.

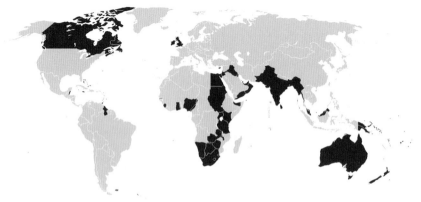

The extent of the British Empire

Trade and industry

Britain continued to be a great trading nation. The government began to promote policies of free trade, abolishing a number of taxes on imported goods. One example of this was the repealing of the Corn Laws in 1846. These had prevented the import of cheap grain. The reforms helped the development of British industry, because raw materials could now be imported more cheaply.

Victorian age railway expansion

Working conditions in factories generally became better. In 1847, the number of hours that women and children could work was limited by law to 10 hours per day. Better housing began to be built for workers.

Transport links also improved, enabling goods and people to move more easily around the country. Just before Victoria came to the throne the father and son George and Robert Stephenson pioneered the railway engine and a major expansion of the railways took place in the Victorian period. Railways were built throughout the Empire. There were also great advances in other areas, such as the building of bridges by engineers such as Isambard Kingdom Brunel.

Isambard Kingdom Brunel (1806-59)

Brunel was originally from Portsmouth, England. He was an engineer who built tunnels, bridges, railway lines and ships. He was responsible for constructing the Great Western Railway which was the first major railway built in Britain. It runs from Paddington Station in London to the south west of England, the West Midlands and Wales. Many of Brunel's bridges are still in use today.

The Clifton Suspension Bridge (above), designed by Isambard Kingdom Brunel (right), spanning the Avon gorge

British Industry led the world in the 19th Century. The UK produced more than half the world's iron, coal and cotton cloth. The UK also became a centre for financial services, including insurance and banking. In 1851, the Great Exhibition opened in Hyde Park in the Crystal Palace, a huge building made of steel and glass. Exhibits ranged from huge machines to handmade goods. Countries from all over the world showed their goods but most of the objects were made in Britain.

The Crimean War

From 1853 to 1856, Britain fought with Turkey and France against Russia in the Crimean War. It was the first war to be extensively covered by the media through news stories and photographs. The conditions were very poor and many soldiers died from illnesses they caught in the hospitals, rather than from war wounds.

Queen Victoria introduced the Victoria Cross medal during this war. It honours acts of valour by soldiers.

Florence Nightingale (1820-1910)
Florence Nightingale was born in Italy to English parents. At the age of 31, she trained as a nurse in Germany. In 1854, she went to Turkey and worked in military hospitals, treating soldiers who were fighting in the Crimean War. She and her fellow nurses improved the conditions in the hospital and reduced the mortality rate. In 1860 she established the Nightingale Training school for nurses at St Thomas' Hospital in London. The school was the first of its kind and still exists today, as to many of the practices that Florence used. She is often regarded as the founder of modern nursing.

Ireland in the 19th century
Conditions in Ireland were not as good as the rest of the UK. Two-thirds of the population still depended on farming to make their living, often on very small

plots of land. Many depended on potatoes as a large part of their diet. In the middle of the century the potato crop failed, and Ireland suffered a famine.

A million people died from disease and starvation. Another million and a half left Ireland. Some emigrated to the Unites States and others came to England.

19th century emigrants

By 1961 there were large populations of Irish people in cities such as Liverpool, London, Manchester and Glasgow.

The Irish Nationalist movement had grown strongly through the 19th century. Some such as the Fenians favoured complete independence. Others, such as Charles Stuart Parnell, advocated 'Home Rule', in which Ireland would remain in the UK but have its own parliament.

The right to vote

As the middle classed in the wealthy industrial towns and cities grew in influence, they began to demand more political power. The Reform Act of 1832 had greatly increased the number of people with the right to vote. The Act also abolished the old pocket ad rotten boroughs and more parliamentary seats were given to the towns and cities. There was a permanent shift of political power from the countryside to the towns but voting was still based on ownership of property. This meant that members of the working class were still unable to vote.

A movement began to demand the vote for the working classes and other people without property. Campaigners, called the Chartists, presented petitions to Parliament. At first they seemed to be unsuccessful, but in 1867 there was another Reform Act. This created many more urban seats in Parliament and reduced the amount of property that people needed to have before they could vote. However, the majority of men still did not have the right to vote and no women could vote.

A Chartist riot

Suffragettes

Politicians realized that the increased number of voters meant that they needed to persuade people to vote for them if they were to be sure of being elected to Parliament. The political parties began to create organisations to reach out to ordinary voters.

Universal suffrage (the right of every adult, male or female, to vote) followed in the next century. In common with the rest of Europe, women in 19th century Britain had fewer rights than men. Until 1870, when a woman got married, her earnings, property and money automatically belonged to her husband. Acts of Parliament in 1870 and 1882 gave wives the right to keep their own earnings and property.

In the late 19th and 20th centuries, an increasing number of women campaigned and demonstrated for greater rights and, in particular, the right to vote. They formed the women's suffrage movement and became known as the 'suffragettes'.

Emmeline Pankhurst (1856-1928)

Emmeline Pankhurst was born in Manchester in 1858. She set up the Women's Franchise League in 1889, which fought to get the vote in local elections for married women. In 1903 she helped found the Women's Social and Political Union (WSPU).

This was the first group whose members were called 'suffragettes'. The group used civil disobedience as part of their protest to gain the votes for women. They chained themselves to railings, smashed windows and committed arson. Many of the women, including Emmeline, went on hunger strike. In 1918, women over the age of 30 were given voting rights and the right to stand for Parliament, partly in recognition of the contribution women made to the war effort during the First World War. Shortly before Emmeline's death in 1928, women were given the right to vote at 21, the same as men

The future of the Empire

Although the British Empire continued to grow until the 1920s, there was already discussion in the late 19th century about its future direction.

Supporters of expansion believed that the Empire benefited Britain through increased trade and commerce. Others thought the Empire had become over-expanded and that the frequent conflicts in many parts of the Empire, such as India's north-west frontier or southern Africa, were a drain on resources. Yet the great majority of British people believed in the Empire as a force for good in the world.

The Boer War

The Boer War of 1899 to 1902 made the discussions about the future of the Empire more urgent. The British went to war in South Africa with settlers from the Netherlands called the Boers.

The Boers fought fiercely and the war went on for more over three years. Many died in the fighting and many more from disease. There was some public sympathy for the Boers and people began to question whether the Empire could continue.

As different parts of the Empire developed, they won greater freedom and autonomy from Britain.

Mafeking, Boer War

Eventually, by the second half of the 20th century, there was, for the most part, an orderly transition from Empire to Commonwealth, with countries being granted their independence.

British Army crossing Tugela River, Boer War

Rudyard Kipling (1865-1936)

Rudyard Kipling was born in India in 1865 and later lived in India, the UK and the USA. He wrote books and poems set in both India and the UK. His poems and novels reflected the idea that the British Empire was a force for good. Kipling was awarded the Nobel Prize in Literature in 1907. His books include the *Just So Stories* and *The Jungle Book,* which continue to popular today.

His poem, *If* has often been voted among the UK's favourite poems. It begins with these words:

'If you can keep your head when all about you
Are losing theirs and blaming it on you;
If you can trust yourself when all men doubt you,
But make allowance for their doubting too;
If you can wait and not be tired of waiting,
Or being lied about, don't deal in lies,
Or being hated, don't give way to hating.
And yet don't look too good, nor talk too wise
(If, Rudyard Kipling)

Check that you understand

- *The change in the balance of power between Parliament and the monarchy.*
- *When and why Scotland joined England and Wales to become Great Britain*
- *The reasons for a rebellion in Scotland led by Bonnie Prince Charlie*
- *The ideas of the Enlightenment*
- *The importance of the Industrial Revolution and development of industry*
- *The slave trade and when it was abolished*
- *The growth of the British Empire*
- *How democracy developed during this period*

THE 20TH CENTURY

The First World War

The early 20th century was a time of optimism in Britain. The nation, with its expansive Empire, well-admired navy, thriving industry and strong political institutions, was what is now known as a global 'superpower'. It was also a time of social progress.

Archduke Franz Ferdinand of Austria - assassinated

Financial help for the unemployed, old-age pensions and free school meals were just a few of the important measures introduced. Various laws were passed to improve safety in the workplace; town planning rules were tightened to prevent the further development of slums; and better support was given to mothers and their children after divorce and separation. Local government became more democratic and a salary for members of Parliament (MPs) was introduced for the first time, making it easier for more people to take part in public life.

World War I British fighter aircraft

This era of optimism and progress was cut short when war broke out between several European nations. On 28 June 1914, Archduke Franz Ferdinand of Austria was assassinated. This set off a chain of events leading to the First World War (1914-18). But while the assassination proved a trigger for war, other factors – such as a growing sense of nationalism in many European states; increasing militarism; imperialism; and the division of the major European powers into two camps – all set the conditions for war.

A British 'dreadnought' battleship

The conflict was centered in Europe, but it was a global war involving nations from around the world. Britain was part of the Allied Powers, which included (amongst

Machine gun emplacement at the Somme

others) France, Russia, Japan, Belgium, Serbia – and later, Greece, Italy, Romania and the United States.

The whole of the British Empire was involved in the conflict – for example more than a million Indians fought on behalf of Britain in lots of different countries, and around 40,000 were killed. Men from the West Indies, Africa, Australia, New Zealand and Canada also fought with the British. The Allies fought against the Central Powers – mainly Germany, the Austro-

Soldiers fighting in the trenches during the First World War

Hungarian Empire, the Ottoman Empire and later Bulgaria. Millions of people were killed or wounded, with more than 2 million British casualties.

One battle, the British attack on the Somme in July 1916, resulted in about 60,000 British casualties on the first day alone.

The First World War ended at 11.00am on 11th November 1918 with victory for Britain and its allies.

The partition of Ireland

In 1913, the British government promised 'Home Rule' for Ireland. The proposal was to have a self-governing Ireland with its own parliament but still part of the UK. A Home Rule Bill was introduced in Parliament. It was opposed by the Protestants in the north of Ireland, who threatened to resist Home Rule by force. The outbreak of the First World War led the British government to postpone any changes in Ireland. Irish Nationalists were not willing to wait and in 1916 there was an uprising (the Easter Rising) against the British in Dublin. The leaders of the uprising were executed under military law. A guerrilla war against the British

army and the police in Ireland followed. In 1921 a peace treaty was signed and in 1922 Ireland became two countries. The six counties in the north which were mainly Protestant remained part of the UK under the name Northern Ireland. The rest of Ireland became the Irish Free State. It had its own government and became a republic in 1949.

Aftermath of the Easter Rising in Dublin

There were people in both parts of Ireland who disagreed with the split between the North and the South. They still wanted Ireland to be one independent country.

Years of disagreement led to a terror campaign in Northern Ireland and elsewhere. The conflict between those wishing for full Irish independence and those wishing to remain loyal to the British government is often referred to as 'The Troubles'.

The inter war period

In the 1920s, many people's living conditions got better. There were improvements in public housing and new homes were built in many towns and cities. However, in 1929, the world entered the 'Great Depression' and some parts of the UK suffered mass unemployment. The effects of the depression of the 1930s were felt differently in different parts of the UK. The traditional heavy industries such as shipbuilding were badly affected but new industries – including the automobile and aviation industries – developed. As prices generally fell, those in work had more money to spend. Car ownership doubled from 1 million to 2 million between 1930 and 1939. In addition many new houses were built. It was also a time of cultural blossoming, with writers such as Graham Greene and Evelyn Waugh prominent.

The Great Depression

The economist John Maynard Keynes published influential new theories of economics. The BBC started radio broadcasts in 1922 and began the world's first regular television service in 1936.

The Second World War

Adolf Hitler came to power in Germany in 1933. He believed that the conditions imposed on Germany by the Allies after the First World War were unfair; he also wanted to conquer more land for the German people. He set about renegotiating treaties, building up arms, and testing Germany's military strength in nearby countries. The British government tried to avoid another war.

Adolf Hitler inspecting German troops during the invasion of Poland, 1939

However, when Hitler invaded Poland in 1939, Britain and France declared war in order to stop his aggression.

The war was initially fought between the Axis powers (fascist Germany and Italy and the Empire of Japan) and the Allies. The main countries on the allied side were the UK, France, Poland, Australia, New Zealand, Canada and the Union of South Africa.

Having occupied Austria and invaded Czechoslovakia, Hitler followed his invasion of Poland by taking control of Belgium and the Netherlands. Then, in 1940 German forces defeated allied troops and advanced through France.

At this time of national crisis, Winston Churchill became Prime Minister and Britain's war leader.

Winston Churchill (1874-1965)

Churchill was the son of a politician and before becoming a Conservative MP in 1900 was a soldier and journalist. In May 1940 he became Prime Minister. He refused to surrender to the Nazis and was an inspirational leader to the British people in a time of great hardship. He lost the general election in 1945 but returned as Prime Minister in 1951. He was an MP until he stood down at the 1964 General Election.

Following his death in 1965, he was given a state funeral. He remains a much-admired figure to this day; and in 2002 was voted the greatest Briton of all time by the public.

During the War, he made many famous speeches including lines which you may still hear:

'I have nothing to offer but blood, toil, tears and sweat'
Churchill's first speech to the House of Commons after he became Prime Minister, 1940

'We shall fight on the beaches,
 we shall fight on the landing grounds
 we shall fight in the fields and in the streets,
 we shall fight in the hills;
 we shall never surrender'
 Speech to the House of Commons during the Battle of Britain, 1940

'Never in the field of human conflict was so much owed by so many to so few'
 Speech to the House of Commons during the Battle of Britain, 1940

As France fell, the British decided to evacuate the British and French soldiers from France in a huge naval operation. Many civilian volunteers in small pleasure and fishing boats from Britain helped the Navy to rescue more than 300,000 men from the beaches around Dunkirk. Although many lives and a lot of equipment were lost, the evacuation was a success and meant that Britain was better able to continue the fight against the Germans. The evacuation gave rise to the phrase 'the Dunkirk spirit'. From the end of June 1940 until the German invasion of the Soviet Union in June 1941, Britain and the Empire stood almost alone against Nazi Germany.

The evacuation of Dunkirk

Hitler wanted to invade Britain, but before sending troops, Germany needed to control the air. The Germans waged an air campaign against Britain, but the British resisted with their fighter planes and eventually won the crucial aerial battle against the Germans called 'the Battle of Britain', in the summer of 1940.

The most important planes used by the Royal Air Force in the Battle of Britain were the Spitfire and the Hurricane – which were designed and built in Britain. Despite this crucial victory, the German air force was able to continue bombing London and other British cities at night-time. This was called the Blitz. Coventry was almost totally destroyed and a great deal of damage was done in other cities, especially in the East End of London. Despite the destruction, there was a strong national spirit of resistance in the UK. The phrase 'the Blitz spirit' is still used today to describe Britons pulling together in the face of adversity.

A Spitfire

The British surrender of Singapore, 1942

At the same time as defending Britain, the British military was fighting the Axis on many other fronts. In Singapore, the Japanese defeated the British and then occupied Burma, threatening India.

The United States entered the war when the Japanese bombed its naval base at Pearl Harbor in December 1941.

That same year, Hitler attempted the largest invasion in history by attacking the Soviet Union. It was a fierce conflict, with huge losses on both sides. German forces were ultimately repelled by the Soviets, and the damage they sustained proved to be a pivotal point in the war.

Allied D-Day landings, 6 June 1944

The allied forces gradually gained the upper hand, winning significant victories in North Africa and Italy. German losses in the Soviet Union, combined with the support of the Americans, meant that the Allies were eventually strong enough to attack Hitler's forces in Western Europe. On 6 June 1944, allied forces landed in Normandy (this event is often referred to as 'D-Day').

Following victory on the beaches of Normandy, the allied forces pressed on through France and eventually into Germany. The Allies comprehensively defeated Germany in May 1945.

The war against Japan ended in August 1945 when the United States dropped its newly developed atom bombs on the Japanese cities of Hiroshima and Nagasaki. Scientists led by Ernest Rutherford, working at Manchester and then Cambridge University were the first to 'split the atom' and took part in the Manhattan project in the United States, which developed the atomic bomb. The war was finally over.

The Hiroshima Atom Bomb

Alexander Fleming (1881-1955)

Born in Scotland, Fleming move to London as a teenager and later qualified as a doctor. He was researching influenza (the 'flu') in 1928 when he discovered penicillin. This was then further developed into a usable drug by the scientists Howard Florey and Ernst Chain. By the 1940s it was in mass production. Fleming won the Nobel Prize in Medicine in 1945. Penicillin is still used to treat bacterial infections today.

Check that you understand
- *What happened during the First World War*
- *The partition of Ireland and the establishment of the UK as it is today*
- *The events of the Second World War*

BRITAIN SINCE 1945

The welfare state

Although the UK had won the war, the country was exhausted economically and the people wanted change. During the war, there had been significant reforms to the education system and people now looked for wider social reforms.

In 1945 the British people elected a Labour government. The new Prime Minister was Clement Attlee, who promised to introduce a welfare state outlined in the Beveridge Report. In 1948, Aneurin (Nye) Bevan, the Minister for Health, led the establishment of the National Health Service (NHS), which guaranteed a minimum standard of health care for all, free at the point of use.

Aneurin Bevan launching the NHS in 1948

A national system of benefits was also introduced to provide 'social security', so that the population would be protected from the 'cradle to the grave'. The government took into public ownership (nationalized) the railways, coal mines and gas, water and electricity supplies.

Burma's Independence day

Another aspect of change was self-government for former colonies.

In 1947, independence was given to nine countries, including India, Pakistan and Ceylon (now Sri Lanka). Other colonies in Africa, the Caribbean and the Pacific achieved independence over the next 20 years.

The UK developed its own atomic bomb and joined the new North Atlantic Treaty Organisation (NATO), an alliance of nations set up to resist the perceived threat of invasion by the Soviet Union and its allies.

Britain had a Conservative government from 1951 to 1964. The 1950s were a period of economic recovery after the war and increasing prosperity for working people.

First successful British Hydrogen bomb test, 1957

The Prime Minister of the day, Harold Macmillan, was famous for his 'wind of change', speech about decolonization and independence for the countries of the Empire.

Clement Attlee (1886-1967)

Clement Attlee was born in London in 1883. His father was a solicitor and, after studying at Oxford University, Attlee became a barrister. He gave this up to do social work in East London and eventually became a Labour MP. He was Winston Churchill's Deputy Prime Minister in the wartime coalition government and became Prime Minister after the Labour Party won the 1945 election. He was Prime Minister from 1945 to 1951 and led the Labour party for 20 years.

Attlee's government undertook the nationalization of major industries (like coal and steel), created the National Health Service and implemented many of Beveridge's plans for a stronger welfare state. Attlee also introduced measures to improve conditions of workers.

William Beveridge (1879-1963)

William Beveridge (later Lord Beveridge) was a
British economist and social reformer. He served
briefly as a Liberal MP and was subsequently the
leader of the Liberals in the House of Lords but is
best known for the 1942 report Social Insurance
and Allied Services (known as the Beveridge
report).

The report was commissioned by the
wartime government in 1941. It recommended
that the government should find ways of fighting the five 'Giant Evils' of Want,
Disease and Ignorance, Squalor and Idleness and provided the basis of the
modern welfare state.

R A Butler

Richard Austen Butler (later Lord Butler) was born in 1902. He became
a Conservative MP in 1923 and held several positions before becoming
responsible for education in 1941. In this role, he oversaw the introduction of
the Education Act 1944 (often called 'The Butler Act', which introduced free
secondary education in England and Wales.

The education system has changed significantly since the Act was introduced,
but the division between primary and secondary schools that it enforced still
remains in most areas of Britain.

Dylan Thomas (1914-53)

Dylan Thomas was a Welsh poet and writer. He often read
and performed his work in public, including for the BBC.
His most well-known works include the radio play *Under
Milk Wood,* first performed after his death in 1954, and
the poem *Do Not Go Gentle into That Good Night*, which
he wrote for his dying father in 1952.

He died at the age of 39 in New York. There are several
memorials to him in his birthplace, Swansea, including a
statue and the Dylan Thomas centre.

Dylan Thomas statue

Migration in post-war Britain

Rebuilding Britain after the Second World War was a huge task. There were labour shortages and the British government encouraged workers from Ireland and other parts of Europe to come to the UK and help with reconstruction. In 1948, people from the West Indies were also invited to come and work.

During the 1950s, there was still a shortage of labour in the UK. Further immigration was therefore encouraged for economic reasons, and many industries advertised for workers from overseas. For example, centres were set up in the West Indies to recruit people to drive buses. Textile and engineering firms from the north of England and the Midlands sent agents to India and Pakistan to find workers.

For about 25 years, people from the West Indies, India, Pakistan and (later) Bangladesh travelled to work and settle in Britain.

Social change in the 1960s

The decade of the 1960s was a period of significant social change. It was known as 'the Swinging Sixties'. There was a growth in British fashion, cinema and popular music. Two well-known pop music groups of the time were 'The Beatles' and 'The Rolling Stones'. People started to become better off and many bought cars and other consumer goods.

It was also a time when social laws were liberalized, for example in relation to divorce and to abortion in England, Wales and Scotland. The position of women in the workplace also improved. It was quite common at the time to ask women to leave their jobs when they got married, but Parliament passed new laws giving women the right to equal pay and made it illegal for employers to discriminate against women because of their gender.

Concorde

The 1960s was also a time of technological progress. Britain and France developed the world's only supersonic commercial airliner, Concorde.

New styles of architecture, including high-rise buildings and the use of concrete and steel, became common.

The number of people migrating from the West Indies, India, Pakistan and what is now Bangladesh fell in the late 1960s because the government passed new laws to restrict immigration to Britain. Immigrants were required to have a strong connection to Britain through birth or ancestry. Even so, during the early 1970s, Britain admitted 28,000 people of Indian origin who had been forced to leave Uganda.

Some great British inventions of the 20th century

Britain has given the world some wonderful inventions. Examples from the 20th century include:

The **television** was developed by Scotsman John Logie Baird (1888-1946) in the 1920s. In 1932 he made the first television broadcast between London and Glasgow.

Radar was developed by Scotsman Sir Robert Watson-Watt (1892-1973), who proposed that enemy aircraft could be detected by radio waves. The first successful radar test took place in 1935.

Working with radar led Sir Bernard Lovell (1913-2012) to make new discoveries in astronomy. The radio telescope he built at **Jodrell Bank** in Cheshire was for many years the biggest in the world and continues to operate today.

A **Turing machine** is a theoretical mathematical device invented by Alan Turing 1 (1912-54), a British mathematician, in the 1930s. The theory was influential in the development of computer science and the modern-day computer.

The Scottish physician and researcher John Macleod (1876-1935) was the co-discoverer of **insulin**, used to treat diabetes.

The structure of the DNA molecule was discovered in 1953 through work at British universities in London and Cambridge. This discovery contributed to many scientific advances, particularly in medicine and fighting crime. Francis Crick (1916-2004), one of those awarded the Nobel Prize for this discovery, was British.

The **jet engine** was developed in Britain in the 1930s by Sir Frank Whittle (1907- 96), a British Royal Air Force engineer officer.

Sir Christopher Cockerell (1910-99), a British inventor, invented the **hovercraft** in the 1950s.

Britain and France developed **Concorde**, the world's only supersonic passenger aircraft. It first flew in 1969 and began carrying passengers in 1976. Concorde was retired from service in 2003.

The **Harrier jump jet,** an aircraft capable of taking off vertically, was also designed and developed in the UK.

In the 1960s, James Goodfellow (1937-) invented the **cash-dispensing ATM** (automatic teller machine) or 'cashpoint'. The first of these was put to use by Barclays Bank in Enfield, north London in 1967.

IVF (in-vitro fertilization) therapy for the treatment of infertility was pioneered in Britain by physiologist Sir Robert Edwards (1925 -) and gynaecologist Patrick Steptoe (1913-88). The world's first 'test tube baby' was born in Oldham Lancashire in 1978.

In 1996, two British scientists, Sir Ian Wilmot (1944-) and Keith Campbell (1912- 2012), led a team which was the first to succeed in **cloning** a mammal, Dolly the sheep. This has led to further research into the possible use of cloning to preserve endangered species and for medical research.

Sir Peter Mansfield (1933-), a British scientist, is the co-inventor of the **MRI (magnetic resonance imaging)** scanner. This enables doctors and researchers to obtain exact and non-invasive images of human internal organs and has revolutionized diagnostic medicine.

The inventor of the **World Wide Web**, Sir Tim Berners-Lee (1955-), is British. Information was successfully transferred via the web for the first time on 25 December 1990.

Problems in the economy in the 1970s

In the late 1970s, the post-war economic boom came to an end. Prices of goods and raw materials began to rise sharply and the exchange rate between the pound and other currencies was unstable. This caused problems with the 'balance of payments'; imports of goods were valued at more than the price paid for exports.

Many industries and services were affected by strikes and this caused problems between the trade unions and the government. People began to argue that the unions were too powerful and that their activities were harming the UK.

The 1970s were also a time of serious unrest in Northern Ireland. In 1972, the Northern Ireland Parliament was suspended and Northern Ireland was directly ruled by the UK government. Some 3000 people lost their lives in the decades after 1969 in the violence in Northern Ireland.

Mary Peters (1939 -)

Born in Manchester, Mary Peters moved to Northern Ireland as a child. She was a talented athlete who won an Olympic gold medal in the pentathlon in 1972. After this, she raised money for local athletics and became the team manager for the women's British Olympic team. She continues to promote sport and tourism in Northern Ireland and was made a Dame of the British Empire in 2000 in recognition of her work.

Europe and the Common market

West Germany, France, Belgium, Italy, Luxembourg and the Netherlands formed the European Economic Community (EEC) in 1957.

At first the UK did not wish to join the EEC but it eventually did so in 1973. The UK is a full member of the European Union but does not use the Euro currency. *[Note that in a referendum held 23 June 2016 the UK voted to leave the EU.]*

Conservative government from 1979 to 1997

Margaret Thatcher, Britain's first woman Prime Minister, led the Conservative government from 1979 to 1990. The government made structural changes to the economy through privatization of nationalized industries and imposed legal controls on trade union powers.

Deregulation saw a great increase in the role of the City of London as an international centre for investments, insurance and other financial services. Traditional industries, such as shipbuilding and coal mining, declined.

In 1982, Argentina invaded the Falkland Islands, a British overseas territory in the South Atlantic. A naval taskforce was sent from the UK and military action led to the recovery of the islands.

Margaret Thatcher (1925-2013)

Margaret Thatcher was the daughter of a grocer from Grantham in Lincolnshire. She trained as a chemist and lawyer. She was elected as a Conservative MP in 1959 and became a cabinet minister in 1970 as the Secretary of State for Education and Science. In 1975 she was elected as Leader of the Conservative Party and so became Leader of the Opposition. Following the Conservative victory in the General Election of 1979, Margaret Thatcher became the first woman Prime Minister of the UK. She was the longest-serving Prime Minister of the 20th century, remaining in office until 1990.

During her premiership, there were a number of important economic reforms in the UK. She worked closely with the United States President, Ronald Reagan, and was one of the first Western leaders to recognise and welcome the changes in the leadership of the Soviet Union which eventually led to the end of the Cold War.

John Major was Prime Minister after Mrs Thatcher, and helped establish the Northern Ireland peace process.

John Major

Roald Dahl (1916-90)

Roald Dahl was born in Wales to Norwegian parents. He served in the Royal Air Force during the Second World War. It was during the 1940s that he began to publish books and short stories. He is most well known for his children's books, although he also wrote for adults. His best known works include *Charlie and the Chocolate Factory* and *George's Marvellous Medicine*. Several of his books have been made into films.

Labour government from 1997 to 2010

In 1997 the Labour Party led by Tony Blair was elected. The Blair government introduced a Scottish Parliament and a Welsh Assembly. The Scottish Parliament has substantial powers to legislate.

Tony Blair

The Welsh Assembly was given fewer legislative powers but considerable control over public services. In Northern Ireland, the Blair government was able to build on the peace process, resulting in the Good Friday Agreement signed in 1998. The Northern Ireland Assembly was elected in 1999 but suspended in 2002. It was not reinstated until 2007. [*Note: suspended once more in January 2017*] Most paramilitary groups in Northern Ireland have decommissioned their arms and are inactive.

Gordon Brown

Gordon Brown took over as Prime Minister in 2007.

Conflicts in Afghanistan and Iraq

Throughout the 1990s, Britain played a leading role in coalition forces involved in the liberation of Kuwait, following the Iraqi invasion in 1990, and the conflict in the former Republic of Yugoslavia.

Since 2000, British armed forces have been engaged in the global fight against international terrorism and against the proliferation of weapons of mass destruction, including operations in Afghanistan as part of the United Nations (UN) mandated 50-nation International Security Assistance Force (ISAF) coalition and at the invitation of the Afghan government. ISAF is working to

ensure that Afghan territory can never again be used as a safe haven for international terrorism, where groups such as Al Qa'ida could plan attacks on the international community.

As part of this ISAF is building up the Afghan National Security Forces and is helping to create a secure environment in which governance and development can be extended. International forces are gradually handing over responsibility for security over to the Afghans, who will have full security responsibility in all provinces by the end of 2014.

Coalition government 2010 onwards

In May 2010, and for the first time in the UK since February 1974, no political party won an overall majority in the General Election.

The Conservative and Liberal parties formed a coalition and the leader of the Conservative Party, David Cameron, became Prime Minister.

David Cameron

[Notes: In May 2015 a Conservative government was elected with David Cameron as Prime Minister.

David Cameron resigned as Prime Minister following the narrow victory of those campaigning to leave the European Union in the referendum held 23 June 2016 (51.9% to 48.1%). He was succeeded as Prime Minister by Theresa May, Conservative.

Following a General Electoin in June 2017 the Conservatives formed a minority government having agreed a confidence and supply arrangement with the Democratic Unionist Party (DUP) of Northern Ireland. Theresa May remained as Prime Minister.]

Check that you understand

- *The establishment of the welfare state*
- *How life in Britain changed in the 1960s and 1970*
- *British inventions in the 20th century (you do not need to remember dates of birth and deaths)*
- *Events since 1979*

Westminster Abbey has been the coronation church since 1066 and is the final resting place of 17 monarchs

A modern thriving society

This section will tell you about aspects of life in the UK today

Chapter contents
- *The UK today*
- *Religion*
- *Customs and traditions*
- *Sport*
- *Arts and culture*
- *Leisure*
- *Places of interest*

THE UK TODAY

The UK today is a more diverse society than it was 100 years ago in both ethnic and religious terms. Post-war immigration means that nearly 10% of the population has a parent or grandparent born outside the UK. The UK continues to be a multinational and multiracial society with a rich and varied culture. This section will tell you about the different parts of the UK and some of the important places. It will also explain some of the UK's traditions and customs and some of the popular activities that take place.

The nations of the UK

UK is located in the north west of Europe. The longest distance on the mainland is from John O'Groats on the north coast of Scotland to Land's End in the south-west corner of England. It is about 870 miles (approximately 1400 kilometres).

Most people live in towns and cities but much of Britain is still countryside. Many people continue to visit the countryside for holidays and for leisure activities such as walking, camping and fishing.

Cities of the UK

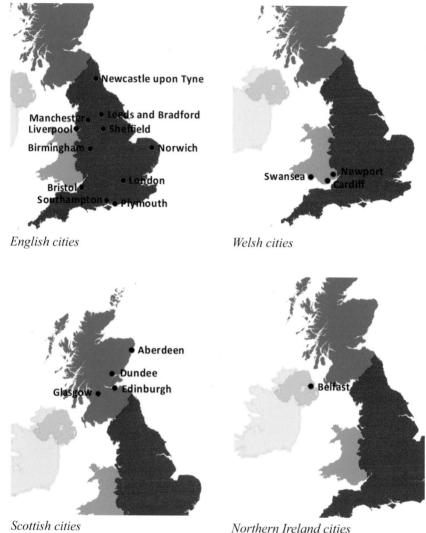

English cities

Welsh cities

Scottish cities

Northern Ireland cities

Capital Cities
- The capital city of the UK is London
- The capital city of Wales is Cardiff
- The capital city of Scotland is Edinburgh
- The capital city of Northern Ireland is Belfast

UK Currency

The currency of the UK is the pound sterling (symbol £).
There are 100 pence to the pound. The denominations
(values) of currency are:

- Coins: 1p, 2p, 5p, 10p, 20p, 50p, £1 and £2

- Notes: £5, £10, £20, £50

Northern Ireland and Scotland have their own banknotes,
which are valid everywhere in the UK. However, shops
and businesses do not have to accept them.

Languages and dialects

There are many variations in language of the different parts of the UK. The
English language has many accents and dialects. In Wales, many people speak
Welsh – a completely different language to English – and it is taught in schools
and universities.

In Scotland, Gaelic (again, a different language) is spoken in some parts of the
Highlands and Islands, and in Northern Ireland some people speak Irish Gaelic.

Population

The table below shows how the population of the UK has changed over time.

Year	UK Population
1600	Just over 4 million
1700	5 million
1801	8 million
1851	20 million
1901	40 million
1951	50 million
1998	57 million
2005	Just under 60 million
2010	Just over 62 million

Source: National statistics

Population growth has been faster in more recent years. Migration into the UK and longer life expectancy have played a part in population growth.

The population is very unequally distributed over the four parts of the UK. England more or less consistently makes up 84% of the total population, Wales around 5%, Scotland just over 8%, and Northern Ireland less than 3%.

An ageing population
People in the UK are living longer than ever before. This is due to improved living standards and better health care. There are now a record number of people aged 85 and over. This has an impact on the cost of pensions and health care.

Ethnic diversity
The UK population is ethnically diverse and changing rapidly, especially in large cities such as London. It is not always easy to get a an exact picture of the ethnic origin of all the population.

There are people in the UK with ethnic origins from all over the world. In surveys, the most common ethnic description chosen is white, which includes most European, Australian, Canadian, New Zealand and American descent. Other significant groups are those of Asian, black and mixed descent.

An equal society
Within the UK, it is a legal requirement that men and women should not be discriminated against because of their gender or because they are, or are not, married. They have equal rights to work, own property, marry and divorce. If they are married, both parents are equally responsible for their children.

Women in Britain toady make up about half of the workforce. On average, girls leave school with better qualifications than boys. More women than men study at university.

Employment opportunities for women are much greater than they were in the past. Women work in all sectors of the economy and there are now women in more high-level positions than ever before, including senior managers, in traditionally male-dominated occupations.
Alongside this, men now work in more varied jobs than they did in the past.

It is no longer expected that women should stay at home and not work. Women often continue to work after having children. In many families today, both partners work and both share responsibility for childcare and household chores.

Check that you understand

- *The capital cities of the UK*
- *What languages other than English are spoken in particular parts of the UK*
- *How the population of the UK has changed*
- *That the UK is an equal society and ethnically diverse*
- *The currency of the UK.*

RELIGION

The UK is historically a Christian country. In the 2009 Citizenship Survey, 70% of people identified themselves as Christian.

Much smaller proportions described themselves as Muslim (4%), Hindu (2%), Sikh (1%), Jewish or Buddhist (both less than 0.5%), and 2% of people followed another religion. This includes Islamic mosques, Hindu temples, Jewish synagogues, Sikh gurdwaras and Buddhist temples. However, everyone has the legal right to choose their religion, or to choose not to practice a religion. In the Citizenship survey, 21% of peoples said they had no religion.

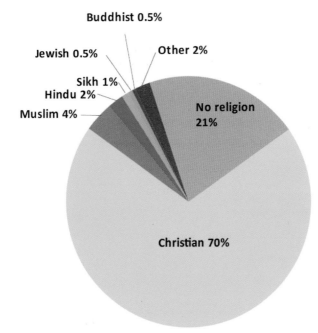

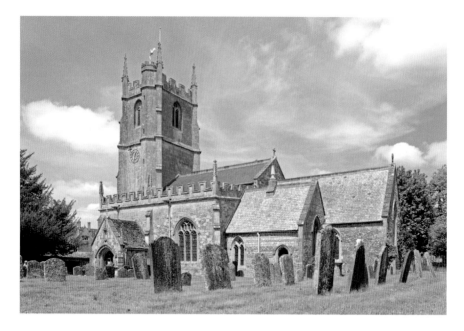

Christian churches

In England, there is a constitutional link between Church and state. The official church of the state is the Church of England (called the Anglican Church in other countries and the Episcopal Church in Scotland and the United States). It is a Protestant Church and has existed since the Reformation in the 1530s.

The monarch is the head of the Church of England. The spiritual leader of the Church of England is the Archbishop of Canterbury. The monarch has the right to select the Archbishop and other senior church officials, but usually the choice is made by the Prime Minister and a committee appointed by the Church. Several Church of England bishops sit in the House of Lords.

In Scotland, the national Church is the Church of Scotland, which is a Presbyterian Church. It is governed by ministers and elders. The chairperson of the General Assembly of the Church of Scotland is the Moderator, who is appointed for one year only and often speaks on behalf of that Church.

There is no established Church in Wales or Northern Ireland.

Other Protestant Christian groups in the UK are Baptists, Methodists, Presbyterians and Quakers. There are also other denominations of Christianity, the biggest of which is Roman Catholic.

Patron saints' days

England, Scotland, Wales and Northern Ireland each have a national saint, called a patron saint. Each saint has a special day:

1 March	St David's Day	Wales
17 March	St Patrick's Day	Northern Ireland
23 April	St George's Day	England
30 November	St Andrew's Day	Scotland

Only Scotland and Northern Ireland have their patron saint's day as an official holiday (although in Scotland not all businesses and offices will close). Events are held across Scotland, Northern Ireland and the rest of the country, especially where there are a lot of people of Scottish, Northern Irish and Irish heritage.

While the patron saints' days are no longer public holidays in England and Wales, they are still celebrated. Parades and small festivals are held all over the two countries.

Check that you understand
* *The different religions that are practiced in the UK*
* *That the Anglican Church, also known as the Church of England, is the Church of the state in England ('the 'established Church')*
* *That other branches of the Christian Church also practice their faith in the UK without being linked to the state*
* *That other religions are practiced in the UK*
* *About the patron saints*

CUSTOMS AND TRADITIONS

The main Christian festivals

Christmas Day, 25 December, celebrates the birth of Jesus Christ. It is a public holiday. Many Christians go to church on Christmas Eve (24 December) or on Christmas day itself.

Christmas is celebrated in a traditional way. People usually spend the day at home and eat a special meal, which often includes roast turkey, Christmas pudding and mince pies. They give gifts, send cards and

Christmas turkey

Father Christmas (Santa Claus)

decorate their houses. Christmas is a special time for children.

Very young children believe that Father Christmas (also known as Santa Claus) brings them presents during the night before Christmas Day. Many people decorate a tree in their home.

Boxing Day is the day after Christmas Day and is a public holiday.

Easter takes place in March or April. It marks the death of Jesus Christ on Good Friday and his rising from the dead on Easter Sunday. Both Good Friday and the following Monday, called Easter Monday, are public holidays.

The 40 days before Easter are known as **Lent**. It is a time when Christians take time to reflect and prepare for Easter. Traditionally, people would fast during this period and today many people will give something up, like a favourite food. The day before Lent stats is called Shrove Tuesday, or Pancake Day. People eat pancakes, which were traditionally made to use up foods such as eggs, fat and milk before fasting. Lent begins in Ash Wednesday. There are church services where Christians are marked with an ash cross on their forehead as a symbol of death and sorrow for sin.

Easter is also celebrated by people who are not religious. 'Easter eggs' are chocolate eggs often given as presents at Easter as a symbol of new life.

Easter eggs

Other religious festivals

Diwali normally falls in October or November and lasts for five days. It is often called the festival of lights. It is celebrated by Hindus and Sikhs. It celebrates the victory of good over evil and the gaining of knowledge. There are different stories about how the festival came about. There is a famous celebration of Diwali in Leicester.

Hannukah is in November or December and is celebrated for eight days. It is to remember the Jews' struggle for religious freedom. On each day of the festival a candle is lit on a stand of eight candles (called a menorah) to remember the story of the festival, where oil that should have lasted only a day did so for eight.

Eid al-Fitr celebrates the end of Ramadan, when Muslims have fasted for a month. They thank Allah for giving them the strength to complete the fast. The date when it takes place changes every year. Muslims attend special services and meals.

Eid ul Adha remembers that the prophet Ibrahim was willing to sacrifice his son when God ordered him to. It reminds Muslims of their own commitment to God. Many Muslims sacrifice an animal to eat during this festival. In Britain this has to be done in a slaughterhouse.

Vaisakhi (also spelled Baisakhi) is a Sikh festival which celebrates the founding of the Sikh community known as the Khalsa. It is celebrated on 14 April each year with parades, dancing and singing.

Other festivals and traditions

New Year, 1 January, is a public holiday. People usually celebrate on the night of 31 December (called New Year's Eve). In Scotland 31 December is called Hogmanay and 2 January is also a public holiday. For some Scottish people, Hogmanay is a bigger holiday.

Valentine's Day, 14 February , is when lovers exchange cards and gifts. Sometimes people send anonymous cards to someone they secretly admire.

April Fool's Day, 1 April, is a day when people play jokes on each other until midday. The television and newspapers often have stories that are April fool jokes.

Mothering Sunday (or Mother's Day) is the Sunday three weeks before Easter. Children send cards or buy gifts for their mothers.

Father's Day is the third Sunday in June. Children send cards or buy gifts for their fathers.

Halloween, 31 October, is an ancient festival and has roots in the pagan festival to mark the beginning of winter. Young people will often dress up in frightening costumes to play 'trick or treat'. People give them treats to stop them playing tricks on them. A lot of people carve lanterns out of pumpkins and put a candle inside.

Bonfire Night, 5 November, is an occasion when people in Great Britain, set off fireworks at home or in special displays. The origin of this celebration was an event in 1605, when a group of Catholics led by Guy Fawkes failed in their plan to kill the Protestant king with a bomb in the Houses of Parliament. [*Note: this is historically incorrect; the group was led by Robert Catesby – Guy Fawkes was in charge of the explosives.*]

Remembrance Day, 11 November, commemorates those who died fighting for the UK and its allies. Originally it commemorated the dead of the First World War, which ended on 11 November 1918. People wear poppies (the red flower found on the battlefields of the First World War). At 11.00am there is a two minute silence and wreaths are laid at the Cenotaph in Whitehall, London. Unveiled in 1920 the Cenotaph is the centerpiece of the Remembrance Day service.

The Cenotaph

Bank holidays

As well as those mentioned previously, there are other public holidays each year called bank holidays, when banks and many other businesses are closed for the day. These are of no religious significance. They are at the beginning of May, in late May or early June and in August. In Northern Ireland, the anniversary of the Battle of the Boyne is also a public holiday.

Check that you understand
- *The main Christian festivals that are celebrated in the UK*
- *Other religious festivals that are important in the UK*
- *Some of the other events that are celebrated in the UK*
- *What a bank holiday is*

SPORT

Sports of all kinds play an important part in many people's lives. There are several sports that are particularly popular in the UK. Many sporting events take place at major stadiums such as Wembley Stadium in London and the Millennium Stadium in Cardiff.

Local governments and private companies provide sports facilities such as swimming pools, tennis courts, football pitches, dry ski slopes and gymnasiums. Many famous sports, including cricket, football, lawn tennis, golf and rugby, began in Britain.

The UK has hosted the Olympic Games on three occasions: 1908, 1948 and 2012. The main Olympic site for the 2012 Games was in Stratford, East London. The British team was very successful, across a wide range of Olympic sports, finishing third in the medal table.

The 2012 London Olympics Stadium

The Paralympic Games for 2012 were also hosted in London. The Paralympics have their origin in the work of Dr Sir Ludwig Guttman, a German refugee, at the Stoke Mandeville Hospital in Buckinghamshire. Dr Guttman developed new methods of treatment for people with spinal injuries and encouraged patients to take part in exercise and sport.

Notable British sportsmen and women

Sir Roger Bannister (1929-) was the first man in the world to run a mile in under four minutes, in 1954.

Sir Jackie Stewart (1939-) is a Scottish former racing driver who won the Formula 1 world championship three times.

Bobby Moore (1941-93) captained the English
football team that won the World Cup in 1966.

Sir Ian Botham (1955-) captained the English cricket
team and holds a number of English Test cricket records,
both for batting and bowling.

Jayne Torvill (1957-) and Christopher Dean (1958-)
won gold medals for ice dancing at the Olympic
Games in 1984 and in four consecutive world
championships.

Sir Steve Redgrave (1962-) won medals in rowing
in five consecutive Olympic Games and is one of
Britain's greatest Olympians.

Baroness Tanni Grey-Thompson (1969-) is an
athlete who uses a wheelchair and won 16 Paralympic
medals including 11 gold medals, in races over five
Paralympic Games. She won the London Marathon
six times and broke total of 30 world records.

Dame Kelly Holmes (1970-) won two gold medals
for running in the 2004 Olympic Games. She has
held a number of British and European records.

Dame Ellen MacArthur (1976-) is a yachtswoman and in 2004 became the fastest person to sail around the world single handed.

Sir Chris Hoy (1976-) is a Scottish cyclist who has won six gold and one silver Olympic medals. He has also won 11 world championship titles.

David Weir (1979-) is a Paralympian who uses a wheelchair and has won six gold medals over two Paralympic Games. He has won the London Marathon six times.

Bradley Wiggins (1980-) is a cyclist. In 2012, he became the first Briton to win the Tour de France. He has won seven Olympic medals, including gold medals in the 2004, 2008 and 2012 Olympic Games.

Mo Farah (1983-) is a British distance runner, born in Somalia. He won gold medals in the 2012 Olympics for the 5,000 and 10,000 metres and is the first Britain to win the Olympic gold in the 10,000 metres.

Jessica Ennis (1986-) is an athlete. She won the 2012 Olympic gold medal in the heptathlon, which includes seven different track and field events. She also holds a number of British athletics records.

Andy Murray (1987-) is a Scottish tennis player who in 2012 won the men's singles in the US Open. He is the first British man to win a singles title in a Grand Slam tournament since 1936. In the same year, he won Olympic gold and silver medals and was runner-up in the men's singles at Wimbledon.

Ellie Simmonds (1994 -) is a Paralympian who won gold medals for swimming at the 2008 and 2012 Paralympic Games and holds a number of world records. She was the youngest member of the British team at the 2008 Games.

Cricket

Cricket originated in England and is now played in many countries. Games can last up to five days but still result in a draw! The idiosyncratic nature of the game and its complex laws are said to reflect the best of the British character and sense of fair play. You may come across expressions such as 'rain stopped play', 'batting on a sticky wicket', 'playing a straight bat', 'bowled a googly' or 'it's just not cricket', which have passed into everyday usage. The most famous competition is the Ashes, which is a series of Test matches played between England and Australia.

Football

Football is the UK's most popular sport. It has a long history in the UK and the first professional football clubs were formed in the late 19th century.

England, Scotland, Wales and Northern Ireland each have separate leagues in which clubs representing different towns and cities compete. The English Premier League attracts a huge international audience. Many of the best players in the world play in the Premier League. Many UK teams also compete in competitions such as the UEFA (Union of European Football Associations) Champions League, against other teams from Europe. Most towns and cities have a professional club and people take great pride in supporting their home team. There can be great rivalry between different football clubs and among fans.

Each country in the UK has its own national team that competes with other national teams across the world in tournaments such as the FIFA (Federation Internationale de Football Association) World Cup and UEFA European Football Championships. England's only tournament victory was at the World Cub of 1966, hosted in the UK. Football is also a popular sport to play in many local communities, with people playing amateur games every week in parks all over the UK.

Rugby
Rugby originated in England in the early 19th century and is very popular in the UK today. There are two different types of rugby, which have different rules: union and league. Both have separate leagues and national teams in England,

Wales, Scotland and Northern Ireland (who play with the Irish Republic). Teams from all countries compete in a range of competitions. The most famous rugby union competition is the Six Nations Championship between England, Ireland, Scotland, Wales, France and Italy. The Super League is the most well-known rugby league (club) competition.

Horse racing
There is a very long history of horse racing in Britain, with evidence of events taking place as far back as Roman times. The sport has a long association with royalty. There are racecourses all over the UK. Famous horse-racing events

include: Royal Ascot, a five day race meeting in Berkshire attended by members of the Royal Family; the Grand National at Aintree near Liverpool; and the Scottish Grand National at Ayr. There is a National Horseracing Museum in Newmarket, Suffolk.

Golf

The modern game of golf can be traced back to 15th century Scotland. It is a popular sport played socially as well as professionally.

There are public and private golf courses all over the UK. St Andrews in Scotland is known as the home of golf.

The Open Championship is the only 'Major' tournament held outside the United States. It is hosted by a different golf course each year.

Tennis

Modern Tennis evolved in England in the late 19th century. The first tennis club was founded in Leamington Spa in 1872. The most famous tournament hosted in Britain is The Wimbledon Championships, which takes place each year at the All England Lawn Tennis and Croquet Club. It is the oldest tennis tournament in the world and the only 'Grand Slam' event played on grass.

Water sports

Sailing continues to be popular in the UK, reflecting our maritime heritage. A British sailor, Sir Francis Chichester, was the first person to sail single-handed around the world, in 1966/67. Two years later, Sir Robin Knox-Johnson became the first person to do this without stopping.

Many sailing events are held throughout the UK, the most famous of which is at Cowes on the Isle of Wight.

Rowing is also popular, both as a leisure activity and as a competitive sport. There is a popular yearly race on the Thames between Oxford and Cambridge Universities.

Motor sports

There is a long history of motor sport in the UK, for both cars and motor cycles. Motor-car racing in the UK started in 1902. The UK continues to be a world leader in the development and manufacture of motor-sport technology.

A Formula 1 Grand Prix event is held in the UK each year and a number of British Grand Prix drivers have won the Formula 1 World Championship. Recent British winners include Damon Hill, Lewis Hamilton and Jenson Button.

Skiing

Skiing is increasingly popular in the UK. Many people go abroad to ski and there are also dry ski slopes throughout the UK. Skiing on snow may also be possible during winter. There are five ski centres in Scotland, as well as Europe's longest dry ski slope near Edinburgh.

ARTS AND CULTURE

Music

Music is an important part of British culture, with a rich and varied heritage. It ranges from classical music to modern pop. There are many different venue and musical events that take place across the UK.

The Proms is an eight-week summer season of orchestral classical music that takes place in various venues, including the Royal Albert Hall, London. It has been organised by the British Broadcasting Corporation (BBC) since 1927. The Last Night of the Proms is the most well-known concert and (along with others in the series) is broadcast on television.

The Royal Albert Hall

93

Classical music has been popular in the UK for many centuries.

Henry Purcell (1659-95) was, the organist at Westminster Abbey. He wrote church music, operas and other pieces, and developed a British style distinct from that elsewhere in Europe. He continues to be influential on British composers.

The German-born composer **George Frederick Handel (1685-1759)** spent many years in the UK and became a British citizen in 1727. He wrote the *Water Music* for King George I and Music for the Royal Fireworks for his son, George II. Both these pieces continue to be very popular. Handel also wrote an oratorio, *Messiah*, which is sung regularly by choirs, often at Easter time.

More recently, important composers include **Gustav Holst (1874-1934)**, whose works include *The Planets*, a suite of pieces themed around the planets of the solar system. He adapted *Jupiter*, part of the Planets suite, as the tune for *I vow to thee my country*, a popular hymn in British churches.

Sir Edward Elgar (1857-1934) was born in Worcester, England. His best-known work is probably the *Pomp and Circumstance Marches. March No 1* (*Land of Hope and Glory*) is usually played at the Last Night of the Proms at the Royal Albert Hall.

Ralph Vaughan Williams (1872-1958) wrote music for orchestras and choirs. He was strongly influenced by traditional English folk music.

Sir William Walton (1902-83) wrote a wide range of music, from film scores to opera. He wrote marches for the coronation of King George VI and Queen Elizabeth II but his best-known works are probably Façade, which became a ballet, and *Balthazar's Feast*, which is intended to be sung by a large choir.

Benjamin Britten (1913-76) is best known for his operas, which include *Peter Grimes* and *Billy Budd*. He also wrote *A Young Person's Guide to the Orchestra*, which is based on a piece of music by Purcell and introduces the listener to the various different sections of an orchestra. He founded the Aldeburgh festival in Suffolk, which continues to be a popular music event of international importance.

Other types of popular music, including folk music, jazz, pop and rock music, have flourished in Britain since the 20th century. Britain has had an impact on popular music around the world, due to the wide use of the English language, the UK's cultural links with many countries, and British capacity for invention and innovation.

Since the 1960s, British pop music has made one of the most important cultural contributions to life in the UK. Bands including The Beatles and The Rolling Stones continue to have an influence on music both here and abroad.

British pop music has continued to innovate – for example, the Punk movement of the late 1970s, and the trend towards boy and girl bands in the 1990s.

There are many large venues that host music events throughout the year, such as: Wembley Stadium, The O2 in Greenwich, south-east London; and the Scottish Exhibition and Conference Centre (SECC) in Glasgow. Festival season takes place across the UK every summer, with major events in various locations. Famous festivals  include Glastonbury, the Isle of Wight Festival and the V Festival. Many bands and solo artists, both well-known and up-and-coming, perform at these events.

The National Eisteddfod of Wales is an annual culture festival which includes music, dance, art and original performances largely in Welsh. It includes a number of important competitions for Welsh poetry.

The Mercury Music Prize is awarded each September for the best album from the UK and Ireland.

The Brit Awards is an annual event that gives awards in a range of categories, such as best British group and best British solo artist.

Theatre

There are theatres in most towns and cities throughout the UK, ranging from the large to the small. They are an important part of local communities and often show both professional and amateur productions. London's West End, also known as 'Theatreland'. Is particularly well known.

The Globe Theatre, London

The Mousetrap, a murder-mystery play by Dame Agatha Christie, has been running in the West End since 1952 and has had the longest initial run of any show in history.

There is also, a strong tradition of musical theatre in the UK. In the 19th century, Gilbert and Sullivan wrote the comic operas, often making fun of popular culture and politics. These operas include *HMS Pinafore, The Pirates of Penzance* and *The Mikado*. Gilbert and Sullivan's work is still often stages by professional and amateur groups. More recently, Andrew Lloyd Webber has written the music for shows which have been popular throughout the world, including in collaboration with Tim Rice, *Jesus Christ Superstar* and *Evita*, and also *Cats* and *The Phantom of the Opera*.

One British tradition is pantomime. Many theatres produce a pantomime at Christmas time. They are based on fairy stories and are light-hearted plays with music and comedy, enjoyed by family audiences. One of the traditional characters is the Dame, a woman played by a man. There is often also a pantomime horse or cow played by two actors in the same costume.

The Edinburgh Festival takes place in Edinburgh, Scotland, every summer. It is a series of different arts and cultural festivals, with the biggest and most well-known being the Edinburgh Festival Fringe ('the Fringe'). The Fringe is a showcase of mainly theatre and comedy performances. It often shows experimental work.

The Laurence Olivier Awards take place annually at different venues in London. There are a variety of categories, including best director, best actor and best actress. The awards are named after the British actor Sir Laurence Olivier, later Lord Olivier, who was best known for his role in various Shakespeare plays.

Art

During the Middle Ages, most art had a religious theme, particularly wall paintings in churches and illustrations in religious books. Much of this was lost after the Protestant Reformation but wealthy families began to collect other paintings and sculptures. Many of the painters working in Britain in the 16th and 17th centuries were from abroad – for example, Hans Holbein and Sir Anthony Van Dyck. British artists, particularly those painting portraits and landscapes, became well known from the 18th century onwards.

Tate Britain Gallery, London

Works by British and international artists are displayed in galleries across the UK. Some of the most well known galleries are The National Gallery, Tate Britain and Tate Modern in London, the National Museum in Cardiff, and the National Gallery of Scotland in Edinburgh.

The National Gallery, London

Notable British Artists

Thomas Gainsborough (1727-88) was a portrait painter who often painted people in country or garden scenery.

David Allan (1744-96) was a Scottish painter who was best known for painting portraits. One of his famous works is called *The Origin of Painting*.

Joseph Turner (1775-1851) was an influential landscape painter in a modern style. He is considered the artist who raised the profile of landscape painting.

John Constable (1776-1837) was a landscape painter most famous for his works of Dedham Vale on the Suffolk-Essex border in the east of England.

The Pre-Raphaelites were an important group of artists in the second half of the 19th century. They painted detailed pictures on religious or literary themes in bright colours.

The group included Holman Hunt, Dante Gabriel Rossetti and Sir John Millais.

Sir John Lavery (1856-1941) was a very successful Northern Irish portrait painter. His work included painting the Royal Family.

Henry Moore (1898-1986) was an English sculptor and artist. He is best known for his large bronze abstract sculptures.

John Petts (1914-91) was a Welsh artist, best known for engravings and stained glass.

Lucian Freud (1922-2011) was a German-born British artist. He is best known for his portraits.

David Hockney (1937-) was an important contributor to the 'pop art' movement of the 1960s and continues to be influential today.

The Turner Prize was established in 1984 and celebrates contemporary art. It was named after Joseph Turner.

Four works are shortlisted every year and shown at Tate Britain before the winner is announced.

The Turner Prize is recognised as one of the most prestigious visual art awards in Europe. Previous winners include Damien Hurst and Richard Wright.

A Henry Moore sculpture

Architecture

The architecture heritage of the UK is rich and
varied. In the Middle Ages, great cathedrals and
churches were built, many of which still stand
today. Examples are the cathedrals of Canterbury
and Salisbury. The White Tower in the Tower of
London is an example of a Norman castle keep,
built on the orders of William the Conqueror.

The White Tower, Tower of London

St Paul's Cathedral, London

Gradually, as the countryside became more peaceful
and landowners became richer, the houses of the
wealthy became more elaborate and great country
houses such as Hardwick Hall in Derbyshire were
built. British styles of architecture began to evolve.

In the 17th century, **Inigo Jones** took inspiration from
classical architecture to design the Queen's House at
Greenwich and the Banqueting House in Whitehall
in London. Later in the century, Sir Christopher
Wren helped develop a British version of the ornate
styles popular in Europe in buildings such as the new
St Paul's Cathedral.

In the 18th century, simpler designs became more popular. The Scottish Architect
Robert Adam influenced the development of architecture in the UK, Europe and
America. He designed the inside decoration as well as the building itself in great
houses such as Dumfries House in Scotland. His ideas influenced architects in
cities such as Bath, where the Royal Crescent was built.

The Royal Crescent, Bath

In the 19th century, the medieval
'gothic' style became popular
again. As cities expanded, many
great public buildings were
built in this style. The Houses
of Parliament and St Pancreas
Station were built at this time, as
were the town halls in cities such
as Manchester and Sheffield.

The Houses of Parliament, London

India Gate, New Delhi, India and the Cenotaph, London were both designed by Sir Edward Lutyens

In the 20th century **Sir Edwin Lutyens** had an influence throughout the British Empire.

He designed New Delhi to be the seat of government in India. After the First World War he was responsible for many war memorials throughout the world, including the Cenotaph in Whitehall.

The Cenotaph is the site of the annual Remembrance Day service attended by the Queen, politicians and foreign ambassadors.

Modern British architects including **Sir Norman Foster, Lord (Richard) Rogers** and **Dame Zaha Hadid** continue to work on major projects throughout the world as well as within the UK.

Alongside the development of architecture, garden design and landscaping have played an important role in the UK. In the 18th century, **Lancelot 'Capability' Brown** designed the grounds around country houses so that the landscape appeared to be natural, with grass trees and lakes. He often said that a place had 'capabilities'. Later, **Gertrude Jekyll** often worked with Edward Lutyens to design colourful gardens around the houses he designed. Gardens continue to be an important part of homes in the UK. The annual Chelsea Flower Show showcases garden design from Britain and around the world.

Fashion and design

Britain has produced many great designers, from Thomas Chippendale (who designed furniture in the 18th century) to Clarice Cliff (who designed Art Deco ceramics) to Sir Terence Conran (a 20th-century interior designer). Leading fashion designers of recent years include Mary Quant, Alexander McQueen and Vivienne Westwood.

Literature

The UK has a prestigious literary history and tradition. Several British writers, including the novelist Sir William Golding, the poet Seamus Heaney, and the playwright Harold Pinter, have won the Nobel Prize in literature. Other authors have become well known in popular fiction. Agatha Christie's detective stories are read all over the world and Ian Fleming's books introduced James Bond. In 2003, The Lord of the Rings by JRR Tolkien was voted the country's best loved novel.

The **Man Booker Prize for Fiction** is awarded annually for the best fiction novel writer written by an author from the Commonwealth, Ireland or Zimbabwe. It has been awarded since 1968. Past winners include Ian McEwan, Hilary Mantel and Julian Barnes.

Notable authors and writers

Jane Austen (1775-1817) was an English novelist. Her books include *Pride and Prejudice* and *Sense and Sensibility*. Her novels are concerned with marriage and family relationships. Many have been made into television programmes or films.

Charles Dickens (1812-70) wrote a number of very famous novels, including *Oliver Twist* and *Great Expectations*.

You will hear references in everyday talk to characters in his books such as *Scrooge* (a mean person) or *Mr Micawber* (always hopeful).

Charles Dickens.

Robert Louis Stevenson (1850-94) wrote books which are still read by adults and children today.

His most famous books include *Treasure Island, Kidnapped* and *Dr Jekyll and Mr Hyde*.

Thomas Hardy (1840-1930) was an author and poet.

His best known novels focus on rural society and include *Far from the Madding Crowd* and *Jude the Obscure*.

Sir Arthur Conan Doyle (1859-1930) was a Scottish doctor and writer.

He was best known for his stories about Sherlock Holmes - one of the first fictional detectives.

Evelyn Waugh (1903-66) wrote satirical novels, including *Decline and Fall* and *Scoop*. He is perhaps best known for *Brideshead Revisited*.

Sir Kinsley Amis (1922-95) was an English novelist and poet. He wrote more than 20 novels. The most well known is *Lucky Jim*.

Graham Greene (1904-91) wrote novels often influenced by his religious beliefs, including *The Heart of the Matter*, *The Honorary Consul*, *Brighton Rock* and *Our Man in Havana*.

J K Rowling (1965-) wrote the Harry Potter series of children's books which have enjoyed huge international success. She now writes fiction for adults as well.

British poets

British poetry is among the richest in the world. The Anglo-Saxon poem Beowulf tells of its hero's battles against monsters and is still translated into modern English. Poems which survive from the Middle Ages include Chaucer's Canterbury Tales and a poem called *Sir Gawain and the Green Knight* about one of the knights at the court of King Arthur.

John Milton

As well as plays, Shakespeare wrote many sonnets (poems which must be 14 lines long) and some longer poems. As Protestant ideas spread, a number of poets wrote poems inspired by their religious views. One of these was John Milton, who wrote *Paradise Lost*.

Other poets, including William Wordsworth, were inspired by nature. Sir Walter Scott wrote poems inspired by Scotland and the traditional stories and songs from the area on the borders of Scotland and England. He also wrote novels, many of which were set in Scotland.

Sir Walter Scott

Poetry was very popular in the 19th century, with poets such as William Blake, John Keats, Lord Byron, Percy Shelley, Alfred Lord Tennyson and Robert and Elizabeth Browning. Later, many poets – for example, Wilfred Owen and Siegfried Sassoon – were inspired to write about experiences in the First World War. Recent, popular poets included Sir Walter de la Mare, John Masefield, Sir John Betjeman and Ted Hughes.

Some of the best-known poets are buried or commemorated in Poet's Corner in Westminster Abbey.

Poet's Corner in Westminster Abbey

Some famous lines include:

'Oh to be in England now that April's there
And whoever wakes in England sees, some mourning unaware,
That the lowest boughs and brushwood sheaf
Round the elm-tree bole are in tiny leaf
While the Chaffinch sings on the orchard bough
In England – Now!
(Robert Browning, 1812-89 – Home Thoughts from Abroad)

She walks in beauty, like the night
Of cloudless climes and starry skies
All that's best of dark and bright
Meet in her aspect and her eyes
(Lord Byron, 1788-1824 – She Walks in Beauty)

I wander'd lonely as a cloud
That floats on high o'er vales and hills
When all at once I saw a crowd,
A host of garden daffodils
(William Wordsworth, 1770-1850)

Tyger! Tyger! Burning bright
In the forests of the night,
What immortal hand or eye
Could frame thy fearful symmetry?
(William Blake, 1757-1827 – The Tyger)

What passing-bells for those who die as cattle?
Only the monstrous anger of the guns.
Only the stuttering rifles' rapid rattle
Can patter out their hasty orisons.
(Wilfred Owen, 1893-1918 – Anthem for Doomed Youth)

Check that you understand
- *Which sports are particularly popular in the UK*
- *Some of the major sporting events that take place every year*
- *Some of the major arts and culture events that happen in the UK*
- *How achievements in arts and culture are formally recognised*
- *Important figures in British literature*

An allotment

LEISURE

People in the UK spend their leisure time in many different ways.

Gardening
A lot of people have gardens at home and will spend their free time looking after them. Some people rent additional land called 'an allotment', where they grow fruit and vegetables. Gardening and flower shows range from national exhibitions to small local events. Many towns have garden centres selling plants and gardening equipment. There are famous gardens to visit throughout the UK, including Kew Gardens, Sissinghurst and Hidcote in England, Crathes Castle and Inveraray Castle in Scotland, Bodnant Garden in Wales and Mount Stewart in Northern Ireland.

The countries that make up the UK all have flowers which are particularly associated with them and which are sometimes worn on national saints days:

The Rose - England

The Daffodil - Wales

The Shamrock - Ireland

The Thistle - Scotland

Shopping

There are many different places to go shopping in the UK. Most towns and cities have a central shopping area, which is called the town centre. Undercover shopping centres are also common – these might be in town centres or on the outskirts of a town or city. Most shops in the UK are open seven days a week, although trading hours on Sundays and public holidays are generally reduced. Many towns also have markets on one or more days a week, where stallholders sell a variety of goods.

Cooking and food

Many people in the UK enjoy cooking. They often invite each other to their homes for dinner. A wide variety of food is eaten in the UK because of the country's rich cultural heritage and diverse population.

Traditional foods

There are a variety of foods that are traditionally associated with different parts of the UK.

 England   Roast beef, which is served with potatoes, vegetables, Yorkshire puddings (batter that is baked in the oven) and other accompaniments. Fish and chips are also popular.

 Wales: Welsh cakes – a traditional Welsh snack made from flour, dried fruits and spices, and served either hot or cold.

 Scotland: Haggis – a sheep's stomach stuffed with offal, suet, onions and oatmeal.

 Northern Ireland: Ulster fry – a fried meal with bacon, eggs, sausage, black pudding, white pudding, tomatoes, mushrooms, soda bread and potato bread.

FILMS

British film industry

The UK has had a major influence on modern cinema.

Films were first shown publicly in the UK in 1896 and film screenings very quickly became popular. From the beginning, British film makers became famous for clever special effects and this continues to be an area of British expertise. From the early days of the cinema, British actors have worked in both the UK and USA. Sir Charles (Charlie) Chaplin became famous in silent movies for his tramp character and was one of many British actors to make a career in Hollywood.

British studios flourished in the 1930s. Eminent directors included Sir Alexander Korda and Sir Alfred Hitchcock, who later left for Hollywood and remained an important film director until his death in 1980. During the Second World War, British movies (for example *In Which We Serve*) played an important part in boosting morale. Later, British directors, including Sir David Lean and Ridley Scott found great success both in the UK and internationally.

Charlie Chaplin

The 1950s and 1960s were a high point for British comedies. Including *Passport to Pimlico, The Ladykillers* and, later, the *Carry On films*.

Many of the films now produced in the UK are made by foreign companies, using British expertise. Some of the most commercially successful films of all time, including the two highest grossing film franchises (*Harry Potter* and *James Bond*), have been produced in the UK. Ealing Studios has a claim to being the oldest continuously working film studio facility in the world. Britain continues to be particularly strong in special effects and animation. One example is the work of Nick Park, who has won four Oscars for his animated films, including three for films featuring *Wallace and Gromit*.

Actors such as Sir Lawrence Olivier, David Niven, Sir Rex Harrsion and Richard Burton starred in a wide variety of popular films. British actors continue to be popular and continue to win awards throughout the world.

Recent British actors to have won Oscars include Colin Firth, Sir Anthony Hopkins, Dame Judi Dench, Kate Winslet and Tilda Swinton.

The annual British Academy Film Awards, hosted by the British Academy of Film and Television Arts (BAFTA), are the British equivalent of the Oscars.

Some famous British films

The 39 Steps (1935), directed by Alfred Hitchcock

Brief Encounter (1945), directed by David Lean

The Third Man (1949), directed by Carol Reed

The Belles of St Trinian's (1954), directed by Frank Launder

Lawrence of Arabia (1962), directed by David Lean

Women in Love (1969), directed by Ken Russell

Don't Look Now (1973), directed by Nicolas Roeg

Chariots of Fire (1981), directed by Hugh Hudson

The Killing Fields (1984), directed by Roland Joffe

Four Weddings and a Funeral (1994), directed by Mike Newell

Touching the Void (2003), directed by Kevin MacDonald

British comedy

The traditions of comedy and satire, and the ability to laugh at ourselves, are an important part of the UK character.

Medieval kings and rich nobles had jesters who told jokes and made fun of people at Court. Later Shakespeare included comic characters in his plays. In the 18th century, political cartoons attacking prominent politicians – and sometimes, the monarch or other members of the Royal Family – became increasingly popular. In the 19th century, satirical magazines began to be published. The most famous was *Punch*, which was published for the first time in the 1840s. Today, cartoons continue to be published in newspapers, and magazines such as *Private Eye* continue the tradition of satire.

Comedians were a popular feature of British music hall, a form of variety theatre which was very common until television became the leading form of entertainment in the UK. Some of the people who had performed in the music halls in the 1940s and 1950s, such as *Morecambe and Wise*, became stars of television.

Television comedy developed its own style. Situation comedies or sitcoms, which often look at family life and relationships in the workplace, remain popular. Satire has also continued to be important, with shows like *That Was The Week That Was* in the 1960s and *Spitting Image* in the 1980s and 1990s. In 1969, *Monty Python's Flying Circus* introduced a new type of progressive comedy. Stand-up comedy, where a solo comedian talks to a live audience, has become popular again in recent years.

Television and radio

Many different television (TV) channels are available in the UK. Some are free to watch and others require a paid subscription. British television shows a wide variety of programmes. Popular programmes include regular soap operas such as *Coronation Street* and *East Enders*. In Scotland some Scotland-specific programmes are shown and there is also a channel with programmes in the Gaelic language. There is a Welsh-language channel in Wales. There are also programmes specific to Northern Ireland and some programmes broadcast in Irish Gaelic.

Everyone in the UK with a TV, computer or other medium which can be used for watching TV must have a TV licence. One licence covers all of the equipment in one home, except when people rent different rooms in a shared house and each has a separate tenancy agreement – those people must each buy a separate licence.

People over 75 can apply for a free TV licence and blind people can get a 50% discount. You will receive a fine of up to £1000 if you watch TV but do not have a TV licence.

The money from TV licenses is used to pay for the British Broadcasting Corporation (BBC). This is a British public service broadcaster providing

BBC Broadcasting House

television and radio programmes. The BBC is the largest broadcaster in the world. It is the only wholly state-funded media organisation that is independent of government. Other UK channels are primarily funded through advertisements and subscriptions.

Social networking

Social networking websites such as Facebook and Twitter are a popular way for people to stay in touch with friends, organise social events and share photos, videos and opinions. Many people use social networking on their mobile phones when out and about.

Pubs and night clubs

Public houses (pubs) are an important part of the UK social culture. Many people enjoy meeting friends in the pub. Most communities will have a 'local' pub that is a natural focal point for social activities. Pub quizzes are popular. Pool and darts are traditional pub games.

To buy alcohol in a pub or night club you must be 18 or over, but people under that age may be allowed in some pubs with an adult. When they are 16, people can drink wine or beer with a meal in a hotel or restaurant (including eating areas in pubs) as long as they are with someone over 18.

Pubs usually open during the day from 11.00am (12 noon on Sundays). Night clubs with dancing and music usually open and close later than pubs. The licensee decides the hours that the pub or night club is open.

Betting and gambling

In the UK, people often enjoy a gamble on sports or other events. There are also casinos in many places.

You have to be 18 to go into betting shops or gambling clubs. There is a National Lottery for draws which are made every week. You can enter by buying a ticket or a scratch card.

People under 16 are not allowed to participate in the National Lottery.

Pets

A lot of people in the UK have pets such as cats or
dogs. They might have them for company or because
they enjoy looking after them. It is against the law to
treat a pet cruelly or to neglect it.

All dogs in public places must wear a collar showing
the name and address of the owner. The owner is responsible for keeping the dog
under control and for cleaning up after the animal in a public place.

Vaccinations and medical treatment of animals are available from veterinary
surgeons (vets). There are charities which may help people who cannot afford to
pay a vet.

PLACES OF INTEREST

The UK has a large network of public footpaths in the countryside. There are
also many opportunities for mountain biking, mountaineering and hill walking.
There are 15 national parks in England, Wales and Scotland. They are areas of
protected countryside that everyone can visit, and where people live, work and
look after the landscape.

There are many museums in the UK, which range from small community
museums to large national and civic collections.

Famous landmarks exist in towns, cities and the countryside throughout the UK.
Most of them are open to the public to view (generally for a charge).

Many parts of the countryside and places of interest are kept open by the National
Trust in England, Wales and Northern Ireland and the National Trust of Scotland.
Both are charities that work to
preserve important buildings,
coastline and the countryside in
the UK.

The National Trust was founded in
1895 by three volunteers. There are
now more than 61,000 volunteers
helping to keep the organisation
running.

*Many places of interest are kept open
by the National Trust*

UK landmarks

Big Ben

Big Ben is the nickname for the great bell of the clock at the Houses of Parliament in London. Many people call the clock Big Ben as well. The clock is over 150 years old and is a popular tourist attraction. The clock tower is named 'Elizabeth Tower' in honour of Queen Elizabeth II's Diamond Jubilee in 2012.

The Eden Project

The Eden Project is located in Cornwall, in the south west of England. Its biomes, which are like giant greenhouses, house plants from all over the world. The Eden Project is also a charity which runs environmental and social projects internationally.

Edinburgh Castle
The Castle is a dominant feature in the skyline in Edinburgh, Scotland. It has a long history, dating back to the early Middle Ages. It is looked after by Historic Scotland, a Scottish government agency.

The Giant's Causeway
Located on the north-east coast of Northern Ireland, the Giant's Causeway is a land formation of columns made from volcanic lava. It was formed about 50 million years ago. There are many legends about the Causeway and how it was formed.

Loch Lomond and the Trossachs National Park

This national park covers 720 square miles (1,865 square kilometers) in the west of Scotland. Loch Lomond is the largest expanse of fresh water in mainland Britain and probably the best-known part of the park.

London Eye

The London Eye is situated on the southern bank of the River Thames and is a ferris wheel that is 443 feet (135 metres) tall. It was originally built as part of the UK's celebration of the new millennium and continues to be an important part of New Year celebrations.

Snowdonia
Snowdonia is a national park in North Wales. It covers an area of 838 square miles (2170 square kilometers). Its most well-know landmark is Snowdon, which is the highest mountain in Wales.

The Tower of London
The Tower of London was first built by William the Conqueror after he became king in 1066. Tours are given by the Yeoman Warders, also known as Beefeaters, who tell visitors about the building's history. People can also see the Crown Jewels there.

The Lake District

The Lake District is England's largest national park. It covers 885 square miles (2292 square kilometers). It is famous for its lakes and mountains and is very popular with climbers, walkers and sailors. The biggest stretch of water is Windermere. In 2007, television viewers voted Wastwater as Britain's favourite view.

Check that you understand
- *Some of the ways in which people in the UK spend their leisure time*
- *The development of British cinema*
- *What the television licence is and how it funds the BBC*
- *Some of the places of interest to visit in the UK*

The UK government, the law and your role

This section will tell you about the UK's democratic system of government and will help you understand your role in the wider community.

Chapter contents
- *The development of British democracy*
- *The British constitution*
- *The government*
- *The UK and international institutions*
- *Respecting the law*
- *Fundamental principles*
- *Your role in the community*

The UK is a parliamentary democracy with the monarch as head of state. This section will tell you about the different institutions which make up this democratic system and explain how you can play a part in the democratic process.

THE DEVELOPMENT OF BRITISH DEMOCRACY

Democracy is a system of government where the whole adult population gets a say. This might be by direct voting or by choosing representatives to make decisions on their behalf.

At the turn of the 19th century, Britain was not a democracy as we know it today. Although there were elections to select members of Parliament (MPs), only a small group of people could vote. They were men who were over 21 years of age and who owned a certain amount of property.

The franchise (that is, the number of people who had the right to vote) grew over the course of the 19th century and political parties began to involve ordinary men and women as members.

In the 1830s and 1840s, a group called the Chartists campaigned for reform. They wanted six changes:
1. For every man to have the vote
2. Elections every year
3. For all regions to be equal in the electoral system

A Chartist riot

117

4. Secret ballots
5. For any man to be able to stand as an MP
6. For MPs to be paid

At the time, the campaign was generally seen as a failure. However, by 1918 most of the reforms had been adopted. The voting franchise was also extended to women over 30, and then in 1928 to men and women over 21. In 1969, the voting age was reduced to 18 for men and women.

THE BRITISH CONSTITUTION

A constitution is a set of principles by which a country is governed. It includes all of the institutions that are responsible for running the country and how their power is kept in check. The constitution also includes laws and conventions. The British constitution is not written down in any single document, and therefore it is described as 'unwritten'. This is mainly because the UK, unlike America or France, has never had a revolution which led permanently to a totally new system of government. Our most important institutions have developed over hundreds of years. Some people believe that there should be a single document, but others believe an unwritten constitution allows for more flexibility and better government.

Constitutional institutions
In the UK, there are several different parts of government. The main ones are:

- the monarchy
- Parliament (The House of Commons and the House of Lords)
- the Prime Minister
- the cabinet
- the judiciary
- the police
- the civil service
- local government

In addition, there are devolved governments in Scotland, Wales and Northern Ireland that have the power to legislate on certain issues.

Whitehall, London - Recognised as the centre of Her Majesty's Government the street is lined with Government departments and ministries

The monarchy

Queen Elizabeth II is the head of state of the UK. She is also the monarch or head of state for many countries in the Commonwealth.

The UK has a constitutional monarchy. This means that the king or queen does not rule the country but appoints the government, which the people have chosen in a democratic election.

The monarch invites the leader of the party with the largest number of MPs, or the leader of a coalition between more than one party, to become Prime Minister and can advise warn and

Queen Elizabeth II, head of state of the UK

encourage, but the decisions on government policies are made by the Prime Minister and cabinet (see the section on 'The government').

The Queen has reigned since her father's death in 1952, and in 2012 she celebrated her Diamond Jubilee (60 years as queen). She is married to Prince Philip, the Duke of Edinburgh. Her eldest son, Prince Charles (the Prince of Wales), is the heir to the throne.

The Queen has important ceremonial roles, such as the opening of the new parliamentary session each year. On this occasion the Queen makes a speech which summarises the government's policies in the year ahead. All Acts of Parliament are made in her name.

The Queen represents the UK to the rest of the world. She receives foreign ambassadors and high commissioners, entertains visiting heads of state, and makes state visits overseas in support of diplomatic and economic relationships with other countries.

The Queen has an important role in providing stability and continuity. While governments and Prime Ministers change regularly, the Queen continues as head of state. She provides a focus for national identity and pride, which was demonstrated through the celebrations of her jubilee.

The National Anthem

The National Anthem of the UK is 'God Save the Queen'. It is played at important national occasions and at events attended by the Queen of the Royal Family. The first verse is:

'God save our gracious Queen!
Long live our noble Queen!
God save the Queen!
Send her victorious,
Happy and glorious,
Long to reign over us,
God save the Queen!'

New citizens swear or affirm loyalty to the Queen as part of the citizenship ceremony.

Oath of allegiance

I (name) swear by Almighty God that on becoming a British citizen, I will be faithful and bear true allegiance to Her Majesty Queen Elizabeth the Second, her Heirs and Successors, according to law.

A new citizenship ceremony

Affirmation of allegiance

I (name) do solemnly, sincerely and truly declare and affirm that on becoming a British citizen, I will be faithful and bear true allegiance to Her Majesty Queen Elizabeth the Second, her Heirs and Successors, according to law.

System of government

The system of government in the UK is a parliamentary democracy. The UK is divided into parliamentary constituencies. Voters in each constituency elect their member of Parliament (MP) in a General Election.

All of the elected MPs form the House of Commons. Most MPs belong to a political party, and the party with the majority of MPs forms the government.

If one party does not get a majority, two parties can join together to form a coalition.

The House of Commons
The House of Commons is regarded as the more important of the two chambers in Parliament because its members are democratically elected. The Prime Minister and almost all the members of the cabinet are members of the House of Commons (MPs). Each MP represents a parliamentary constituency, which is a small area of the country. MPs have a number of different responsibilities. They:

The chamber of the House of Commons

- Represent everyone in their constituency
- Help to create new laws
- Scrutinize and comment on what the government is doing
- Debate important national issues

The House of Lords
Members of the House of Lords, known as peers, are not elected by the people and do not represent a constituency. The role and membership of the House of Lords has changed over the last 50 years.

The chamber of the House of Lords

Until 1958, all peers were:
- 'Hereditary, which means they inherited their title
- Senior judges, or
- Bishops of the Church of England

Since 1958, the Prime Minister has had the power to nominate peers just for their own lifetime. These are called life peers. They have usually had an important career in politics, business, law or another profession. Life peers are appointed by the monarch on the advice of the Prime Minister. They also include people nominated by the leaders of the main political parties or by an independent Appointments Commission for non-party peers. Since 1999, hereditary peers have lost the automatic right to attend the House of Lords. They now elect a few of their number to represent them in the House of Lords.

The House of Lords is normally more independent of the government than the House of Commons. It can suggest amendments or propose new laws, which are then discussed by MPs. The House of Lords checks laws that have been passed by the House of Commons to ensure they are fit for purpose. It also holds the government to account to make sure that it is working in the best interests of the people. There are peers who are specialists in particular areas, and their knowledge is useful in making and checking laws. The House of Commons has powers to overrule the House of Lords, but these are not used often.

The Speaker

Debates in the House of Commons are chaired by the Speaker. This person is the chief officer of the House of Commons.

The Speaker is neutral and does not represent a political party, even though he or she is an MP, represents a constituency and deals with constituents' problems like any other MP. The Speaker is chosen by other MPs in a secret ballot.

The Speakers chair

The Speaker keeps order during political debates to make sure the rules are followed. This includes making sure the opposition (see the section on 'The government') has a guaranteed amount of time to debate issues which it chooses. The Speaker also represents Parliament on ceremonial occasions.

Elections

UK Elections

MPs are elected at a General Election, which is held at least every five years.

If an MP dies or resigns, there will be a fresh election, called a by-election, in his or her constituency.

MPs are elected through a system called 'first past the post'. In each constituency, the candidate who gets the most votes is elected. The government is usually formed by the party that wins the majority of constituencies. If no party wins a majority, two parties may join together to form a coalition.

Voting

European parliamentary elections

Elections for the European Parliament are also held every five years. Elected members are called members of the European Parliament (MEPs).

Elections to the European Parliament use a system of proportional representation, where seats are allocated to each party in proportion to the total number of votes it has won.

Contacting elected members

All elected members have a duty to serve and represent their constituents. You can get contact details for all your representatives and their parties from your local library and from www.parliament.uk.

MPs, Assembly members, members of the Scottish Parliament (MSPs) and MEPs are also listed in The Phone Book, published by BT and Yellow Pages.

You can contact MPs by letter or telephone at their constituency office, or at their office in the House of Commons: The House of Commons, Westminster, London SW1A 0AA, telephone 020 7729 3000.

In addition, many MPs, Assembly members, MSPs and MEPs hold regular local 'surgeries', where constituents can go in person to talk about issues that are of concern to them. These surgeries are often advertised in the local newspaper.

Check that you understand
- *How democracy has developed in the UK*
- *What a constitution is and how the UK's constitution is different from those of most other countries*
- *The role of the monarch*
- *The role of the House of Commons and the House of Lords*
- *What the Speaker does*
- *How the UK elects MPs and MEPs*

THE GOVERNMENT

The Prime Minister
The Prime Minster (PM) is the leader of the political party in power. He or she appoints the members of the cabinet and has control over many important public appointments. The official home of the Prime Minister is 10 Downing Street, in central London, near the Houses of Parliament. He or she also has a country house outside London called Chequers.

The cabinet
The Prime Minister appoints about 20 senior MPs to become ministers in charge of departments. These include:

- Chancellor of the Exchequer – responsible for the economy
- Home Secretary – responsible for crime, policing and immigration
- Foreign Secretary – responsible for managing relationships with foreign countries
- Other ministers (called 'Secretaries of State') responsible for subjects such as education, health and defence.

These ministers form the cabinet, a committee which usually meets weekly and makes important decision about government policy. Many of these decisions have to be debated or approved by Parliament. Each department also has a number of other ministers, called Ministers of State and Parliamentary Under-Secretaries of State, who take charge of particular areas of the department work.

The cabinet meeting room

The opposition
The second largest party in the House of Commons is called the opposition. The leader of the opposition usually becomes the Prime Minister if his or her party wins the next General Election. The leader of the opposition leads his or her party in pointing out what they see as the government's failures and weaknesses. One important opportunity to do this is at Prime Minister's Questions, which takes place every week while Parliament is sitting. The leader of the opposition appoints senior opposition MPs to be 'shadow ministers'. They form the shadow cabinet and their role is to challenge the government and put forward alternative policies.

The party system

Anyone aged 18 or over can stand for election as an MP but they are unlikely to win unless they have been nominated to represent one of the major political parties. These are the Conservative Party, the Labour Party, the Liberal Democrats, or one of the parties representing Scottish, Welsh or Northern Irish

interests. There are a few MPs who do not represent any of the main political parties. They are called 'independents' and usually represent an issue important to the constituency.

The main political parties actively look for members of the public to join their debates, contribute to their costs, and help at elections for Parliament or for local government. They have branches in most constituencies and hold policy-making conferences every year.

Pressure and lobby groups are organisations which try to influence government policy. They play an important role in politics. Some are representative organisations such as the CBI (Confederation of British Industry), which represent the views of British businesses. Others campaign on particular topics, such as the environment (for example, Greenpeace) or human rights (for example, Liberty).

The civil service

Civil servants support the government in developing and implementing its policies. They also deliver public services. Civil servants are accountable to ministers. They are chosen on merit and are politically neutral – they are not

political appointees. People can apply to join the civil service through and application process, like other jobs in the UK.

Civil servants are expected to carry out their role with dedication and a commitment to the civil service and its core values. These are: integrity, honesty, objectivity and impartiality (including being politically neutral).

Civil servants meeting with members of the armed forces

Local government

Towns, cities and rural areas in the UK are governed by democratically elected councils, often called 'local authorities'. Some areas have both district and county councils, which have different functions. Most large towns and cities have a single local authority.

Local authorities provide a range of services in their areas. They are funded by money from central government and by local taxes.

Many local authorities appoint a mayor, who is the ceremonial leader of the council. In some towns, a mayor is elected to be the effective leader of the administration. London has 33 local authorities, with the Greater London Authority and the Mayor of London coordinating policies across the capital. For most local authorities, local elections for councilors are held in May every year. Many candidates stand for council election as members of a political party.

London City Hall - Home of the London Assembly and the Mayor of London

Devolved administrations

Since 1997, some powers have been devolved from the central government to give people in Wales, Scotland and Northern Ireland more control over matters that directly affect them. There is also a Northern Ireland Assembly, although this has been suspended on a few occasions.

Policy and laws governing defence, foreign affairs, immigration, taxation and social security all remain under central UK government control. However, many other public services, such as education, are controlled by the devolved administrations

The devolved administrations each have their own civil service.

The Welsh government

The Welsh government and National Assembly for Wales are based in Cardiff, the capital city of Wales. The National Assembly has 60 Assembly members (AMs) and elections are held every four years using a form of proportional representation Members can speak in either Welsh or English, and all of the Assembly's publications are in both languages.

The Welsh Assembly has the power to make laws for Wales in 20 areas, including:

* Education and Training
* Health and Social Services
* Economic Development
* Housing

Since 2011, the National Assembly for Wales has been able to pass laws on these topics without the agreement of the UK Parliament.

The National Assembly for Wales

The Scottish Parliament

The Scottish Parliament was formed in 1999. It sits in Edinburgh, the capital city of Scotland.

There are 129 members of the Scottish Parliament (MSPs), elected by a form of proportional representation. The Scottish Parliament can pass laws for Scotland on all matters which are not specifically reserved to the UK Parliament. The matters on which the Scottish Parliament can legislate include:

* Civil and criminal law
* Health
* Education
* Planning
* Additional tax-raising powers

The Scottish Parliament

The Northern Ireland Assembly

A Northern Ireland Parliament was established in 1922, when Ireland was divided, but it was abolished in 1972, shortly after the Troubles broke out in 1969.

The Northern Ireland Assembly was established soon after the Belfast Agreement (or Good Friday Agreement) in 1998. There is a power-sharing agreement which distributes ministerial offices amongst the main parties. The Assembly has 108 elected members, known as MLAs (members of the Legislative Assembly). They are elected with a form of proportional representation.

The Northern Ireland Assembly can make decisions on issues such as:

- Education
- Agriculture
- The Environment
- Health
- Social Services

The Northern Ireland Assembly building known as Stormont

The UK government has the power to suspend all devolved assemblies. It has used this power several times in Northern Ireland when local political leaders found it difficult to work together. However, the Assembly has been running successfully since 2007.

[Note: the Northern Ireland Assembly was suspended again in January 2017]

The Media and government

Proceedings in Parliament are broadcast on television and published in official reports called Hansard. Written reports can be found in large libraries and at www.parliament.uk. Most people get information about political issues and events from newspapers (often called 'the press'), television, radio and the internet.

The UK has a free press. This means that what is written in newspapers is free from government control. Some newspaper owners and editors hold strong political opinions and run campaigns to try to influence government policy and public opinion. By law, radio and television coverage of the political parties must be balanced and so equal time has to be given to rival viewpoints.

Check that you understand

- *The role of the Prime Minister, cabinet, opposition and shadow cabinet.*
- *The role of political parties in the UK system of government*
- *Who the main political parties are*
- *What pressure and lobby groups do*
- *The role of the civil service*
- *The role of local government*
- *The powers of the devolved governments in Wales, Scotland and Northern Ireland*
- *How proceedings in Parliament are recorded*
- *The role of the media in keeping people informed about political issues*

Who can vote?

The UK has had a fully democratic voting system since 1928. The present voting age of 18 was set in 1969 and (with few exceptions) all UK-born and naturalized adult citizens have the right to vote.

Adult citizens of the UK, and citizens of the Commonwealth and the Irish Republic who are resident in the UK, can vote in all public elections.

Adult citizens of other EU states who are resident in the UK can vote in all elections except General Elections. *[Note: the voting rights of EU citizens might change following the EU referendum of 23 June 2016 when the UK voted to leave the European Union]*

The electoral register

To be able to vote in a parliamentary, local or European election, you must have your name on the electoral register.

If you are able to vote, you can register by contacting your local council electoral registration office. This is usually based at your local council (in Scotland it may be based elsewhere). If you don't know which local authority you come under, you can find out by visiting www.aboutmyvote.co.uk and entering your postcode. You can also download voter registration forms in English, Welsh and some other languages.

The electoral register is updated every year in September or October. An electoral registration form is sent to every household and this has to be completed and returned with the names of everyone who is resident in the household and eligible to vote.

In Northern Ireland a different system operates. This is called 'individual registration' and all those entitled to vote must complete their own registration form. Once registered, people stay on the register provided their personal details do not change. For more information see the Electoral Office for Northern Ireland website at www.eoni.org.uk.

By law, each local authority has to make its electoral register available for anyone to look at, although this has to be supervised. The register is kept at each local electoral registration office (or council office in England and Wales). It is also possible to see the register at some public buildings such as libraries.

Where to vote?

People vote in elections at places called polling stations, or polling places in Scotland. Before the election you will be sent a poll card. This tells you where your polling station or polling place is and when the election will take place. On election day, the polling station or place will be open from 7.00am until 10.00pm.

When you arrive at the polling station, the staff will ask for your name and address. In Northern Ireland you will also have to show photographic identification. You will then get your ballot paper, which you take to a polling booth to fill in privately.

A polling station

You should make up your own mind who to vote for. No one has the right to make you vote for a particular candidate. You should follow the instructions on the ballot paper. Once you have completed it, put it in the ballot box.

If it is difficult for you to get to a polling station or polling place, you can register for a postal ballot. Your ballot paper will be sent to your home before the election. You then fill it in and post it back. You can choose to do this when you register to vote.

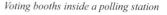

Voting booths inside a polling station

Standing for office

Most citizens of the UK, the Irish Republic or the Commonwealth aged 18 or over can stand for public office. There are some exceptions, including:

- Members of the armed forces
- Civil Servants
- People found guilty of certain criminal offences

Members of the House of Lords may not stand for election to the House of Commons but are eligible for all other public offices.

Visiting Parliament and the devolved administrations

UK Parliament
The public can listen to debates in the Palace of Westminster from public galleries in both the House of Commons and the House of Lords.

You can write to your local MP in advance to ask for tickets or you can queue on the day at the public entrance. Entrance is free. Sometimes there are long queues for the House of Commons and people have to wait for at least one or two hours. It is usually easier to get in to the House of Lords. You can find further information on the UK Parliament website at www.Parliament.uk

Northern Ireland Assembly
In Northern Ireland elected members, known as MLAs, meet in the Northern Ireland Assembly at Stormont, in Belfast. There are two way to arrange a visit to Stormont. You can either contact the Education Service (details are on the Northern Ireland Assembly website at www.niassembly.gov.uk) or contact an MLA.

Scottish Parliament
In Scotland the elected members, called MSPs, meet in the Scottish Parliament building at Holyrood in Edinburgh (for more information see www.scottish.parliament.uk). You can get information, book tickets or arrange tours through visitor services. You can write to them at the Scottish Parliament, sp.bookngs@scottish.parliament.uk

National Assembly for Wales
In Wales the elected members, known as AMs, meet in the Welsh Assembly in the Senedd in Cardiff Bay (for more information, see www.wales.gov.uk).
The Senedd is an open building. You can book guided tours or seats in the public galleries for the Welsh Assembly.

To make a booking contact the Assembly Booking Service on 08451 010 5500 or email assembly.bookings@wales.gsi.gov.uk

Check that you understand
- *Who is eligible to vote*
- *How to register to vote*
- *How to vote*
- *Who can stand for public office*
- *How you can visit Parliament, the Northern Ireland Assembly, the Scottish Parliament and the Welsh Assembly*

THE UK AND INTERNATONAL INSTITUTIONS

The Commonwealth

The Commonwealth is an association of countries that support each other and work together towards shared goals in democracy and development.

Most member states were once part of the British Empire, although a few countries which were not have also joined.

The Queen is the ceremonial head of the Commonwealth which currently has 54 member states (listed below). Membership is voluntary.

The Commonwealth has no power over its members, although it can suspend membership. The Commonwealth is based on the core values of democracy, good government and the rule of law

Commonwealth members			
Antigua	Australia	The Bahamas	Bangladesh
Barbados	Belize	Botswana	Brunei
Darussalam	Canada	Cyprus	Dominica
Fiji (suspended)	The Gambia	Ghana	Grenada
Guyana	India	Jamaica	Kenya
Kiribati	Lesotho	Malawi	Malaysia
Maldives	Malta	Mauritius	Mozambique
Namibia	Nauru	New Zealand	Nigeria
Pakistan	Papua New Guinea	Rwanda	Samoa
Seychelles	Sierra Leone	Singapore	Solomon Islands
South Africa	Sri Lanka	St Kitts and Nevis	St Lucia
St Vincent and the Grenadines	Swaziland	Tanzania	Tonga
Trinidad and Tobago	Tuvalu	Uganda	UK
Vanuatu	Zambia		

Note: The Gambia left the Commonwealth in 2013. Fiji's membership was reinstated in 2014.

The European Union

The European Union (EU), originally called the European Economic Community (EEC) was set up by six western European countries (Belgium, France, Germany, Italy, Luxembourg and the Netherlands) who signed the Treaty of Rome on 25 March 1957.

The UK originally decided not to join this group but became a member in 1973.

There are now 28 EU member states.
Croatia became a member state in 2013.

EU member states			
Austria	Belgium	Bulgaria	Croatia
Cyprus	Czech Republic	Denmark	Estonia
Finland	France	Germany	Greece
Hungary	Ireland	Italy	Latvia
Lithuania	Luxembourg	Malta	Netherlands
Poland	Portugal	Romania	Slovakia
Slovenia	Spain	Sweden	UK

EU law is legally binding in the UK and all the other EU member states. European laws are called directives, regulations or framework decisions.

[Note: the UK voted to leave the EU in a referendum held 23 June 2016]

The Council of Europe

The Council of Europe is separate from the EU. It has 47 member countries, including the UK, and is responsible for the protection and promotion of human rights in those countries.

It has no power to make laws but draws up conventions and charters, the most well-known of which is the European Convention on Human Rights and Fundamental Freedoms, usually called the European Convention of Human Rights.

The United Nations

The UK is part of the United Nations (UN), an international organisation with more than 190 countries as members.

The UN was set up after the Second World War and aims to prevent war and promote international peace and security. There are 15 members on the UN Security Council, which recommends action when there are international crises and threats to peace. The UK is one of five permanent members of the Security Council.

The North Atlantic Treaty Organisation (NATO)

The UK is also a member of NATO. NATO is a group of European and North American countries that have agreed to help each other if they come under attack. It also aims to maintain peace between all of its members.

Check that you understand

* *What the Commonwealth is and its role*
* *Other international organisations of which the UK is a member*

RESPECTING THE LAW

One of the most important responsibilities of all residents in the UK is to know and obey the law. This section will tell you about the legal system in the UK and some of the laws that may affect you. Britain is proud of being a welcoming country, but all residents, regardless of background, are expected to comply with the law and to understand that some things which may be allowed in other legal systems are not acceptable in the UK. Those who do not respect the law should not expect to be allowed to become permanent residents in the UK. The law is relevant to all areas of life in the UK. You should make sure that you are aware of the laws which affect your everyday life, including both your personal and business affairs.

The law in the UK

Every person in the UK receives equal treatment under the law. This means that the law applies in the same way to everyone, no matter how they are or where they are from.

Laws can be divided into criminal law and civil law.

Criminal law relates to crimes, which are usually investigated by the police or another authority such as a council, and which are punished by the courts.

Civil law is used to settle disputes between individuals or groups.

Examples of criminal laws	
Carrying a weapon	It is a criminal offence to carry a weapon of any kind, even if it is for self defence. This includes a gun, a knife, or anything that is made or adapted to cause injury.
Drugs	Selling or buying drugs such as heroin, cocaine, ecstasy and cannabis is illegal in the UK.
Racial crime	It is a criminal offence to cause harassment, alarm or distress to someone because of their religion or ethnic origin.
Selling tobacco	It is illegal to sell tobacco products (for example, cigarettes, cigars, roll up tobacco) to anyone under the age of 18.
Smoking in public places	It is against the law to smoke tobacco products in nearly every enclosed public space in the UK. There are signs displayed to tell you where you cannot smoke.
Buying alcohol	It is a criminal offence to sell alcohol to anyone who is under 18 or to buy alcohol for people who are under the age of 18. (There is one exception: people aged 16 or over can drink alcohol with a meal in a hotel or restaurant.)
Drinking in public	Some places have alcohol-free zones where you cannot drink in public. The police also confiscate alcohol or move young people on from public places. You can be fined or arrested.

This list does not include all crimes. There are many that apply in most countries, such as murder, theft and assault. You can find out more about types of crime in the UK at www.gov.uk.

Examples of civil laws	
Housing law	This includes disputes between landlords and tenants over issues such as repairs and eviction.
Consumer rights	An example of this is a dispute about faulty goods or services.
Employment law	These cases include disputes over wages and cases of unfair dismissal or discrimination in the workplace.
Debt	People might be taken to court if they owe money to someone.

The police and their duties

The job of the police in the UK is to:

1. Protect life and property
2. Prevent disturbances
   (also known as keeping the peace)
3. Prevent and detect crime

The police are organised into a number of separate police forces headed by Chief Constables. They are independent of the government.

In November 2012, the public elected Police and Crime Commissioners (PCCs) in England and Wales. These are directly elected individuals who are responsible for the delivery of an efficient and effective police force that reflects the needs of their local communities. PCCs set local priorities and the local policing budget. They also appoint the local Chief Constable.

The police force is a public service that helps and protects everyone, no matter what their background or where they live. Police officers must themselves obey the law. The must not misuse their authority, make a false statement, be rude or abusive, or commit racial discrimination. If police officers are corrupt or misuse their authority they are severely punished.

Police officers are supported by police community support officers (PCSOs). PCSOs have different roles according to the area but usually patrol the streets, work with the public, and support police officers at crime scenes and major events.

All people in the UK are expected to help the police prevent and detect crimes whenever they can. If you are arrested and taken to a police station, a police officer will tell you the reason for your arrest and you will be able to seek legal advice.

If something goes wrong, the police complaints system tries to put it right. Anyone can make a complaint about the police by going to a police station or writing to the Chief Constable of the police force involved. Complaints can be made to an independent body: the Independent Police Complaints Commission in England and Wales, the Police Complaints Commissioner for Scotland or the Police Ombudsman for Northern Ireland.

Terrorism and extremism

The UK faces a range of terrorist threats. The most serious of these is from Al Qa'ida, its affiliates and like-minded organisations. The UK also faces threats from other kinds of terrorism, such as Northern Ireland-related terrorism.

Tavistock Square on the day of the London bombings, 7 July 2005

All terrorist groups try to radicalize and recruit people to their cause. How, where and to what extent they try to do so will vary. Evidence shows that these groups attract very low levels of public support, but people who want to make their homes in the UK should be aware of this threat. It is important that all citizens feel safe. This includes feeling save from all kinds of extremism (vocal or active opposition to fundamental British values), including religious extremism and far-right extremism.

If you think someone is trying to persuade you to join an extremist or terrorist cause, you should notify your local police force.

Check that you understand

- *The difference between the civil and criminal court and some examples of each*
- *The duties of the police*
- *The possible terrorist threats facing the UK*

THE ROLE OF THE COURTS

The judiciary

Judges (who are together called 'the judiciary') are responsible for interpreting the law and ensuring that trials are conducted fairly. They government cannot interfere with this.

Sometimes the actions of the government are claimed to be illegal. If the judges agree then, the government must either change its policies or ask Parliament to change the law. If judges find that a public body is not respecting someone's legal rights, they can order that body to change its practices and/or pay compensation.

Judges also make decisions in disputes between members of the public or organisations. These might be about contracts, property or employment rights or after an accident.

Criminal Courts

There are some differences between the court systems in England and Wales, Scotland and Northern Ireland.

Magistrates' and Justice of the Peace Courts

In England, Wales and Northern Ireland, most minor criminal cases are dealt with in a Magistrates' Court. In Scotland, minor criminal offences go to a Justice of the Peace Court.

Wirral Magistrate's Court

Magistrates and Justices of the Peace (JPs) are members of the local community. In England, Wales and Scotland they usually work unpaid and do not need legal qualifications. They receive training to do the job and are supported by a legal adviser.

Magistrates decide the verdict in each case that comes before them and, if the person is found guilty, the sentence that they are given.

In Northern Ireland, cases are heard by a District Judge or Deputy District Judge, who is legally qualified and paid.

Crown Courts and Sheriff Courts

In England, Wales and Northern Ireland, serious offences are tried in front of a judge and jury in a Crown Court. In Scotland, serious cases are heard in a Sheriff Court with either a sheriff or a sheriff with a jury. The most serious cases in Scotland, such as murder, are heard at a High Court with a judge and jury. A jury is made up of members of the public chosen at random from the local electoral register. In England, Wales and Northern Ireland a jury has 12 members, and in Scotland a jury has 15 members. Everyone who is summoned to do jury service must do it unless they are not eligible (for example because they have a criminal conviction) or they provide a good reason to be excused, such as ill health.

Kingston Crown Court

The jury has to listen to the evidence presented at the trial and then decide a verdict of 'guilty' or 'not guilty' based on what they have heard. In Scotland, a third verdict of 'not proven' is also possible. If the jury finds a defendant guilty the judge decides on the penalty.

Youth Courts

In England, Wales and Northern Ireland, if an accused person is aged 10 to 17, the case is normally heard in a Youth Court in front of up to three specially trained magistrates or a District Judge. The most serious cases will go to the Crown Court. The parents or carers of the young person are expected to attend the hearing. Members of the public are not allowed in Youth Courts, and the name or photographs of the accused young person cannot be published in newspapers or used by the media.

Balham Youth Court

In Scotland, a system called the Children's Hearings System is used to deal with children and young people who have committed an offence.

Northern Ireland has a system of youth conferencing to consider how a child should be dealt with when they have committed an offence.

Civil Courts

County Courts

County Courts deal with a wide range of civil disputes. These include people trying to get back money that is owed to them, cases involving personal injury, family matters, breaches of contract, and divorce. In Scotland, most of these matters are dealt with in the Sheriff Court.

More serious civil cases – for example, when a large amount of compensation is being claimed – are dealt with in the High Court of England, Wales and Northern Ireland.

In Scotland, they are dealt with in the Court of Session in Edinburgh.

Reading County Court

The small claims procedure

The small claims procedure is an informal way of helping people to settle minor disputes without spending a lot of time and money using a lawyer. This procedure is used for claims of less than £5,000 in England and Wales and £3,000 in Scotland and Northern Ireland.

The hearing is held in front of a judge in an ordinary room, and people from both sides of the dispute sit around the table.

Small claims can also be issued online through Money Claims Online (www.moneyclaim.gov.uk).

You can get details about the small claims procedure from your local County Court or Sheriff Court. Details of your local court can be found as follows.

- England and Wales: at www.gov.uk
- Scotland: at www.scotcourts.gov.uk
- Northern Ireland: at www.courtsni.gov.uk

Legal advice

Solicitors
Solicitors are trained lawyers who give advice
on legal matters, take action for their clients and
represent their clients in court.

There are solicitors' offices throughout the UK. It is important to find out which
aspect of law a solicitor specializes in and to check that they have the right
experience to help you with your case. Many advertise in local newspapers and in
Yellow Pages. The Citizens Advice Bureau (www.citizensadvice.org.uk) can give
you names of local solicitors and which areas of law they specialize in. You can
also get this information from the Law Society (www.lawsociety.org.uk) or the
Law Society of Northern Ireland (www.lawsoc-ni.org).

Solicitors charges are usually based on how much time they spend on a case.
It is very important to find out at the start how much a case is likely to cost.

Check that you understand
- *The role of the judiciary*
- *About the different criminal courts in the UK*
- *How you can settle a small claim*

FUNDAMENTAL PRINCIPLES

Britain has a long history of respecting an individual's rights and ensuring
essential freedoms. These rights have their roots in Magna Carta, the Habeas
Corpus Act and the Bill of Rights of 1689, and they have developed over a period
of time. British diplomats and lawyers had an important role in drafting the
European Convention on Human Rights and Fundamental Freedoms. The UK
was one of the first countries to sign the Convention in 1950.

Some of the principles included in the European Convention on Human Rights
are;
- Right to life
- Prohibition of torture
- Prohibition of slavery and forced labour
- Right to liberty and security
- Right to a fair trial
- Freedom of thought, conscience and religion
- Freedom of expression (speech)

The Human Rights Act 1998 incorporated the European Convention on Human Rights into UK law. The government, public bodies and the courts must follow the principles of the Convention.

Equal opportunities

UK laws ensure that people are not treated unfairly in any area of life or work because of their age, disability, sex, pregnancy and maternity, race, religion or belief, sexuality or marital status. If you face problems with discrimination, you can get more information from the Citizens Advice Bureau or from one of the following organisations:

- **England and Wales:** Equality and Human Rights Commission (www.equalityhumanrights.com)

- **Scotland: Equality and Human Rights Commission in Scotland** (www.equality humanrights.com/Scotland/the-commission-in-Scotland) and Scottish Human Rights Commission (www.ScottishHumanRights.com)

- **Northern Ireland:** Equality Commission for Northern Ireland (equalityni.org) Northern Ireland Human Rights Commission (www.nihrc.org)

Domestic violence

In the UK, brutality and violence in the home is a serious crime. Anyone who is violent towards their partner – whether they are a man or a woman, married or living together – can be prosecuted. Any man who forces a woman to have sex, including a woman's husband, can be charged with rape.

It is important for anyone facing domestic violence to get help as soon as possible. A solicitor or the Citizens Advice Bureau can explain the available options. In some areas there are safe places to go and stay in, called refuges or shelters. There are emergency telephone numbers in the helpline section at the front of Yellow Pages, including, for women, the number of the nearest women's centre. You can also phone the 24-hour National Domestic Violence Freephone Helpline on 0808 2000 247 at any time, or the police can help you find a safe place to stay.

Female genital mutilation

Female genital mutilation (FGM), also known as cutting or female circumcision, is illegal in the UK. Practising FGM or taking a girl or woman abroad for FGM is a criminal offence.

Forced marriage

A marriage should be entered into with the full and free consent of both people involved. Arranged marriages, where both parties agree to the marriage are acceptable in the UK.

Forced marriage is where one or both parties do not or cannot give their consent to enter into the partnership. Forcing another person to marry is a criminal offence.

Forced Marriage Protection Orders were introduced in 2008 for England, Wales and Northern Ireland under the Forced Marriage (Civil Protection) Act 2007. Court orders can be obtained to protect a person from being forced into a marriage, or to protect a person in a forced marriage. Similar Protection Orders were introduced in Scotland in November 2011.

A potential victim, or someone acting for them, can apply for an order. Anyone found to have breached an order can be jailed for up to two years for contempt of court.

TAXATION

Income Tax

People in the UK have to pay tax on their income, which includes:

- Wages from paid employment
- Profits from self-employment
- Taxable benefits
- Pensions
- Income from property, savings and dividends.

Money raised from income tax pays for government services such as roads, education and the armed forces.

For most people, the right amount of income tax is automatically taken from their income from employment by their employer and paid directly to HM Revenue & Customs (HMRC), the government department that collects taxes. This system is called 'Pay As You Earn' (PAYE).

If you are self-employed you need to pay your own tax through a system called 'self-assessment', which includes completing a tax return. Other people may also need to complete a tax return.

If HMRC sends you a tax return, it is important to complete and return the form as soon as you have all the necessary information.

You can find out more about income tax at www.hmrc.gov.uk/incometax. You can get help and advice about taxes and completing tax forms from the HMRC self-assessment helpline, on 0845 300 0627, and the HMRC website at www.hmrc.gov.uk

National Insurance
Almost everybody in the UK who is in paid work, including self-employed people, must pay National Insurance Contributions.

The money raised from National Insurance Contributions is used to pay for state benefits and services such as the state retirement pension and the National Health Service.

Employees have their National Insurance Contributions deducted from their pay by their employer. People who are self-employed need to pay National Insurance Contributions themselves.

Anyone who does not pay enough National Insurance Contributions will not be able to receive certain contributory benefits such as Jobseeker's Allowance or a full state retirement pension. Some workers, such as part-time workers may not qualify for statutory payments such as maternity pay if they do not earn enough.

Further guidance about National Insurance Contributions is available on HMRC's website at www.hmrc.gov.uk/ni

Getting a National Insurance Number

A National Insurance Number is a unique personal account number. It makes sure that National Insurance Contributions and tax you pay are properly recorded against your name. All young people in the UK are sent a National Insurance number just before their 16th birthday.

The Department for Work and Pensions

A non-UK national living in the UK and looking for war, stating work or setting up as self-employed will need a National Insurance number. However, you can start work without one. If you have permission to work in the UK, you will need to telephone the Department for Work and Pensions (DWP) to arrange to get a National Insurance Number. You may be required to attend an interview. The DWP will advise you which documents you will need to bring to an interview if one is necessary. You will usually need documents that prove your identity and that you have permission to work in the UK. A National Insurance number does not on its own prove to an employer that you have the right to work in the UK. You can find out more information about how to apply for a National Insurance number at www.gov.uk.

DRIVING

In the UK, you must be at least 17 years old to drive a car or motor cycle and you must have a driving licence to drive on public roads. To get a UK driving licence you must pass a driving test, which tests both your knowledge and practical skills. You need to be at least 16 years old to ride a moped, and there are other age requirements and special tests for driving large vehicles.

Drivers can use their driving licence until they are 70 years old. After that, the licence is valid for 3 years at a time.

In Northern Ireland, a newly qualified driver must display an 'R' plate (for restricted driver) for one year after passing the test.

If your driving licence is from a country in the European Union (EU), Iceland, Liechtenstein or Norway, you can drive in the UK for as long as your licence is valid. If you have a licence from any other country, you may use it in the UK for up to 12 months. To continue driving after that, you must get a full UK driving licence.

If you are resident in the UK, your car or motor cycle must be registered at the Driver and Vehicle Licensing Agency (DVLA). You must pay an annual road tax and display the tax disc, which shows that the tax has been paid, on the windscreen. You must also have valid motor insurance. It is a serious criminal offence to drive without insurance. If your vehicle is over three years old, you must take it for a Ministry of Transport (MOT) test every year. It is an offence not to have an MOT certificate if your vehicle is more than three years old. You can find out more about vehicle tax and MOT requirements from www.gov.uk.

Check that you understand
- *The fundamental principles of UK law*
- *That domestic violence, FGM and forced marriage are illegal in the UK*
- *The system of income tax and National Insurance*
- *The requirements for driving a car*

YOUR ROLE IN THE COMMUNITY

Becoming a British Citizen or settling in the UK brings responsibilities but also opportunities. Everyone has the opportunity to participate in their community. This section looks at some of the responsibilities of being a citizen and gives information about how you can help to make your community a better place to live and work.

Values and responsibilities
Although Britain is one of the world's most diverse societies, there is a set of shared values and responsibilities that everyone can agree with. These values and responsibilities include:

- To obey and respect the law
- To be aware of the rights of others and respect those rights
- To treat others with fairness
- To behave responsibly
- To help and protect your family

- To respect and preserve the environment
- To treat everyone equally, regardless of sex, race, religion, age, disability, class or sexual orientation
- To work to provide for yourself and your family
- To help others
- To vote in local and national government elections

Taking on these values and responsibilities will make it easier for you to become a full and active citizen.

Being a good neighbour

When you move into a new house or apartment, introduce yourself to the people who live near you. Getting to know your neighbours can help you to become part of the community and make friends.

Your neighbours are also a good source of help – for example, they may be willing to feed your pets if you are away, or offer advice on local shops and services.

You can help prevent any problems and conflicts with your neighbours by respecting their privacy and limiting how much noise you make. Also try to keep your garden tidy, and only put your refuse bags and bins on the street or in communal areas if they are due to be collected.

Getting involved in local activities

Volunteering and helping your community are an important part of being a good citizen. They enable you to integrate with other people. It helps make your community a better place if residents support each other. It also helps you to fulfill your duties a citizen, such as behaving responsibly and helping others.

A village fete

147

HOW YOU CAN SUPPORT YOUR COMMUNITY

There are a number of positive ways in which you can support your community and be a good citizen.

Jury service

As well as getting the right to vote, people on the electoral role are randomly selected to serve on a jury.

Anyone who is on the electoral register and is aged 18 to 70 can be asked to do this.

Jury box where the jury sit in court

Helping in schools

If you have children, there are many ways in which you can help at their schools. Parents can often help in classrooms, by supporting activities or listening to children read.

Many schools organise events to raise money for extra equipment or out-of-school activities. Activities might include book sales, toy sales or bringing food to sell. You might have good ideas of your own for raising money.

Sometimes events are organised by parent-teacher associations (PTAs). Volunteering to help with their events or joining the association is a way of doing something good for the school and also making new friends in your local community. You can find out about these opportunities from notices in the school or notes your children bring home.

School governors and school boards

School governors, or members of the school board in Scotland, are people from the local community who wish to make a positive contribution to children's education.

They must be 18 or over at the date of their election or appointment. There is no upper age limit.

Governors and school boards have an important part to play in raising school standards. They have three key roles:

1. Setting the strategic direction of the school
2. Ensuring accountability
3. Monitoring and evaluating school performance

You can contact your local school to ask if they need a new governor or school board member. In England, you can also apply online at the School Governors' One Stop Shop at www.sgoss.org.uk

In England, parents and other community groups can apply to open a free school in their local area. More information about this can be found on the Department for Education Website at www.dfe.gov.uk

Supporting political parties

Political parties welcome new members. Joining one is way to demonstrate your support for certain views and to get involved in the democratic process.

Political parties are particularly busy at election times. Members work hard to persuade people to vote for their candidates, for instance, by handing out leaflets in the street or by knocking on people's doors and asking for their support. This is called 'canvassing'. You don't have to tell a canvasser how you intend to vote if you don't want to.

British citizens stand for office as a local councillor, a member of Parliament (or the devolved equivalents) or a member of the European Parliament. This is an opportunity to become even more involved in political life in the UK.

You may also be able to stand for office if you are an Irish citizen, an eligible Commonwealth citizen or (except for standing as an MP) a citizen of another European country. You can find out more about joining a political party from the individual party websites.

Helping with local services

There are opportunities to volunteer with a wide range of local service providers, including local hospitals and youth projects. Services often want to involve local people in decisions about the way they work.

Universities, housing associations, museums and arts councils may advertise for people to serve as volunteers in their governing bodies.

You can volunteer with the police, and become a special constable or a lay (non-police) representative. You can also apply to become a magistrate. You will find advertisements for vacancies in your local newspaper or on local radio. You can also find out more about these sorts of roles at www.gov.uk

Blood and organ donation

Donated blood is used by hospitals to help people with a wide range of injuries and illnesses. Giving blood takes about an hour to do. You can register to give blood at:

- England and North Wales: www.blood.co.uk
- Rest of Wales: www.welsh-blood.org.uk
- Scotland: www.scotblood.co.uk
- Northern Ireland: www.nibts.org

Many people in the UK are waiting for organ transplants. If you register to be an organ donor, it can make it easier for your family to decide whether to donate your organs when you die. You can register to be an organ donor at www.organdonation.nhs.uk. Living people can also donate a kidney.

Other ways to volunteer

Volunteering is working for good causes without payment. There are many benefits to volunteering, such as meeting new people and helping make your community a better place.

Some volunteer activities will give you a chance to practise your English or develop work skills that will help you find a job or improve your curriculum vitae (CV). Many people volunteer simply because they want to help other people.

Activities you can do as a volunteer include:	
Working with animals	for example, caring for animals at a local rescue shelter
Youth work	for example, volunteering at a youth group
Helping to improve the environment	for example, participating in a litter pick-up in the local area
Working with the homeless	in, for example, a homelessness shelter
Mentoring	for example, supporting someone who has just come out of prison
Work in health and hospitals	for example, working on an information desk in an hospital
Helping older people	at, for example, a residential care home

There are thousands of active charities and voluntary organisations in the UK. They work to improve the lives of people, animals and the environment in many different ways. They range from the British branches of international organisations, such as the British Red Cross, to small local charities working in particular areas. They include charities working with older people (such as Age UK), with children (for example, the National Society for the Prevention of Cruelty to Children (NSPCC)), and with the homeless (for example, Crisis and Shelter). There are also medical research charities (for example, Cancer Research UK), environmental charities (including the National Trust and Friends of the Earth) and charities working with animals (such as the People's Dispensary for Sick Animals (PDSA)).

Volunteers are needed to help with their activities and to raise money. The charities often advertise in local newspapers, and most have websites that include information about their opportunities. You can get information about volunteering for different organisations from www.do-it.org.uk.

There are many opportunities for younger people to volunteer and receive accreditation which will help them to develop their skills. These include the National Citizen Service programme, which gives 16- and 17-year olds the opportunity to enjoy outdoor activities, develop their skills and take part in a community project. You can find out more about these opportunities as follows:

- National Citizen Service: at nationalcitizenservice.direct.gov.uk
- England: at www.www.vinspired.com
- Wales: at www.gwirvol.org
- Scotland: at www.vds.org.uk
- Northern Ireland: at www.volunteernow.co.uk

LOOKING AFTER THE ENVIRONMENT

It is important to recycle as much of your waste as you can. Using recycled materials to make new products uses less energy and means that we do not need to extract more raw materials from the earth. It also means that less rubbish is created, so the amount being put into landfill is reduced.

You can learn more about recycling and its benefits at www.recyclenow.com. At this website you can also find out what you can recycle at home and in the local area if you live in England. This information is available for Wales at www.wasteawarenesswales.org.uk, for Scotland at www.recycleforscotland.com and for Northern Ireland from your local authority.

A good way to support your local community is to shop for products locally where you can. This will help businesses and farmers in your area and in Britain. It will also reduce your carbon footprint, because the products you buy will not have travelled so far.

Walking and using public transport to get around when you can is also a good way to protect the environment. It means that you create less pollution than when you use a car.

Check that you understand
- *The different ways you can help at your child's school*
- *The role of school governors and members of school boards and how you become one*
- *The role of members of political parties*
- *The different local services people can volunteer to support*
- *How to donate blood and organs*
- *The benefits of volunteering for you, other people and the community*
- *The types of activities that volunteers can do*
- *How you can look after the environment*

The Elizabeth Tower of the Houses of Parliament

Revision Material

To help with your study this section of the book includes:

A list of 'Statements that are True' taken from each of the sections. These will help you see if you've picked up key points from the official study material.

A 'Practice Test' to give you an idea of the types of questions that you are likely to encounter in the actual test. The answers are found on the page immediately after the test.

A list of all the people mentioned in the study material. This is presented broadly in the order that they are first mentioned together with a note on who they are.

A table of the all the conflicts mentioned in the study material together with a note on the conflict concerned.

A list of all the battles mentioned in the study material together with a note on who was involved.

A list of the annual calendar events included in the study material.

A list of all the legislation and documents mentioned in the study material.

A historical timeline of the UK based on the study material. *Note that any kings marked with an asterix (*) are not mentioned in the study material.*

Remember that there really is no substitute for reading through the official study material if you want to pass the test first time.

Make sure that you answer all the questions in the real test. If you are not sure 'guess' - you might be lucky.

Good luck with your revision.

Statements that are True

Remember that all of the following statements are TRUE and based on the official study material

What is the UK?
1. 'Great Britain' refers only to England, Scotland and Wales
2. The UK is governed by the parliament sitting in Westminster

A long and illustrious history

Early Britain
1. Julius Caesar led an unsuccessful Roman invasion of Britain in 55BC.
2. The Romans built roads, public buildings, created a structure of law and introduced now plants and animals.
3. Boudicca, Queen of the Iceni, was one of the tribal leaders who fought against the Romans
4. The languages spoken by the Jutes, Angles and Saxon tribes of northern Europe are the basis of modern day English.
5. From AD789 Vikings from Denmark and Norway raided coastal towns and take away goods and slaves.
6. In 1066 the Normans invaded England led by William the Duke of Normandy.
7. The Norman Conquest was the last successful foreign invasion of England

The Middle Ages
1. Edward 1 built huge castles, including Conwy and Caernarvon, in Wales to maintain his power.
2. By 1200 the English ruled an area of Ireland known as the Pale, around Dublin
3. The Normans used a system of land ownership known as feudalism
4. After the Black Death there were labour shortages and peasants began to demand higher wages.
5. In England parliaments were called when the king needed to consult the nobles or raise money.
6. By 1400, in England, official documents were written in English and English had become the preferred language of the royal court and Parliament.
7. In 1455, a civil war started to decide who should be king of England
8. King Richard III of the House of York was killed in the battle of Bosworth Field

The Tudors and Stuarts

1. Henry VIII established the Church of England when the Pope refused him permission to divorce his first wife.
2. Henry VIII was succeeded by his protestant son Edward VI
3. The English defeated the Spanish Armada which had been sent by Spain to Conquer England and restore Catholicism in 1588
4. Sir Francis Drake was one of the first to sail right around the world in his ship the Golden Hind.
5. Elizabeth I never married or had children so when she died in 1603 her heir was her cousin James VI of Scotland.
6. James I and his son Charles I both believed in the 'Divine Right of Kings'
7. Those who supported the king were called 'Cavaliers' and those who supported Parliament 'the Roundheads'.
8. The Scots had not agreed to the execution of Charles I and declared his son Charles II to be king.

A Global Power

1. The laws passed after the Glorious Revolution are the beginning of what is called a 'constitutional monarchy'.
2. Scottish Jacobites attempted to put James II on the throne but were defeated.
3. During the 'Highland Clearances' many Scottish landlords destroyed small farms (crofts) to make space for sheep and cattle.
4. The Bessemer process for mass production of steel led to the development of shipbuilding and railways.
5. William Wilberforce played an important part in changing the law on slavery.
6. In the American War of Independence (1760s) 13 American colonies declared their independence and defeated the British army.
7. The union flag consists of the cross of St George; the cross of St Andrew and the cross of St Patrick.
8. In 1847 the number of hours that women and children could work was limited by law to 10 hours a day.

The 20th century

1. There were more than 2 million British casualties in the First World War
2. In 1922 Ireland became two countries with Northern Ireland remaining part of the UK.
3. When Adolf Hitler of Germany invaded Poland in 1939, Britain and France declared war.
4. 'I have nothing to offer but blood, toil, tears and sweat' is a famous line from a Winston Churchill speech against the Germans.

5. The bombing of London and other cities during the Second World War was called 'The Blitz'
6. The German forces which invaded the Soviet Union in 1941 were ultimately repelled by the Soviets and this proved to be the turning point in the war.
7. British scientists such as Ernest Rutherford took part in the Manhattan Project which developed the Atom Bomb.

Britain since 1945
1. The National Health Service guarantees a minimum standard of care for all, free at the point of use.
2. The UK joined the North Atlantic Treaty Organisation (NATO) - *in 1949*
3. Dylan Thomas was a Welsh poet and writer who wrote the radio play Under Milk Wood.
4. For about 25 years people from West Indies, Pakistan and (later) Bangladesh travelled to work and settle in Britain.
5. During the early 1970s Britain admitted 28,000 people of Indian origin who had been forced to leave Uganda.
6. The jet engine was invented by Sir Frank Whittle
7. Mary Peters was an athlete who won an Olympic medal in the pentathlon in 1972.
8. John Major was Prime Minister after Margaret Thatcher and helped establish the Northern Ireland peace process.

A modern thriving society

The UK today
1. The capital city of Scotland is Edinburgh
2. In Wales many people speak Welsh
3. England makes up 84% of the population; Scotland just over 8%, Wales around 5% and Northern Ireland less than 3%.
4. Women in Britain make up about half of the total workforce

Religion
1. The official Church of the state is the Church of England (Anglican church) which is Protestant
2. The chairperson of the Church of Scotland is the Moderator and is appointed for one year only
3. St Andrew is the patron saint of Scotland and St Andrew's day is 30 November
4. Very young children believe that Father Christmas brings them presents.

5. The day before Easter starts is called Shrove Tuesday or Pancake Day
6. Eid al-Fitr celebrates the end of Ramadan when Muslims have fasted for a month.
7. April Fool's Day, 1 April is a day when people play jokes on each other until midday.
8. Bonfire Night, 5 November is when people set off fireworks to celebrate the failure of plotter including Guy Fawkes to kill the Protestant king with a bomb in the Houses of Parliament.

Sport
1. Bobby Moore captained the English Football team that won the World Cup in 1966
2. Cricket originated in England.
3. England's only international tournament victory was at the World Cup of 1966 hosted in the UK
4. Famous race horsing events include Royal Ascot, the Grand National and the Scottish Grand National
5. Modern tennis evolved in England in the late 19th century.
6. A Formula 1 Grand Prix is held in the UK each year.

Arts and culture
1. Composer Gustav Holst wrote *The Planets*
2. Composer Benjamin Britten is best known for his operas which include *Peter Grimes* and *Billy Bud.*
3. The Pantomime is a British tradition with shows based on fairy stories and light-hearted plays.
4. Thomas Gainsborough was a portrait painter who painted people in country or garden scenery.
5. David Hockney was an important contributor to 'pop' art of the 1960s
6. Sir Christopher Wren developed St Paul's Cathedral
7. In the 18th century Lancelot 'Capability' Brown designed the grounds around country houses.
8. Leading fashion designers include Mary Quant, Alexander McQueen and Vivienne Westwood

Leisure
1. The thistle is associated with the country of Scotland
2. Most shops open 7 days a week although trading hours on Sundays and public holidays are greatly reduced.

3. Ulster fry is a traditional Northern Ireland food
4. Some of the most commercially successful films of all time, including film franchises James Bond and Harry Potter, have been produced in the UK
5. In the 18th century political cartoons attacking politicians, the monarchy and Royal Family became popular.
6. The British Broadcasting Corporation is a British public service broadcaster providing television and radio programmes.
7. At 16 people can drink wine or beer with a meal in a hotel or restaurant as long as they are with someone over 18.
8. All dogs in public places must wear a collar showing the name and address of the owner.

Places of interest
1. The Eden Project in Cornwall is a charity which runs environmental and social projects internationally
2. Loch Lomond is the largest expanse of fresh water in mainland Britain.
3. The Lake District is England's largest national park and is famous for its lakes and mountains.

The UK Government and your role

The development of British democracy
1. Women over the age of 30 gained the right to vote and stand for election to Parliament in 1918

The British Constitution
1. The UK has a constitutional monarchy which means that the king or queen does not rule the country but appoints the government.
2. The National Anthem of the UK is 'God Save the Queen'
3. The party with the majority of MPs forms the government.
4. Until 1958 all peers were 'hereditary', senior judges or bishops of the Church of England
5. The Speaker is neutral and does not represent a political party.
6. Elections to the European Parliament are held every 5 years

The government
1. The Home Secretary is responsible for crime, policing and immigration.
2. Prime Minister's Questions takes place every week while Parliament is sitting.

3. MPs who do not represent any of the main political parties are 'Independents'
4. Towns, cities and rural areas are governed by democratically elected councils.
5. There are 129 members of the Scottish Parliament (MSPs) elected by proportional representation.
6. The Northern Ireland Assembly can make decisions on education, agriculture, the environment, health and social services.
7. All UK-born and naturalised adult citizens have the right to vote (with a few exceptions)

The UK and international institutions
1. The Commonwealth is based on the core values of democracy, good government and the rule of law.
2. EU laws are called directives, regulations or framework decisions.
3. The UN was set up after the Second World War to prevent war and promote international peace and security.
4. The Council of Europe is responsible for the protection and promotion of human rights in member countries.

Respecting the law
1. Civil law is used to settle disputes between individuals or groups.
2. It is illegal to sell tobacco to anyone under the age of 18.
3. Example of areas of civil law include Housing Law, Consumer Rights, Employment Law and Debt.
4. PCCs are directly elected Police and Crime Commissioners and are responsible for delivery of an efficient and effective police force.

The role of the courts
1. Judges also make decisions in disputes between members of the public or organisations such as contract, property or employment rights disputes.
2. Magistrates decide the verdict and, if the person is found guilty, the verdict they are given.
3. In England, Wales and Northern Ireland a jury has 12 members.
4. In Scotland a jury has 15 members.
5. In England, Wales and Northern Ireland if an accused person is aged 10 to 17 the case is normally heard in a Youth Court.
6. The jury has to listen to the evidence presented at the trial and decide a verdict of 'guilty' or 'not guilty' based on what they have heard.
7. In Scotland a verdict of 'not proven' is possible at jury trials.
8. Solicitors charges are usually based on how much time they spend on a case.

Fundamental principles

1. If you face problems with discrimination you can get more information from the Citizens Advice Bureau or the Equality and Human Rights Commission.
2. Female genital mutilation (FGM) also known as cutting or female circumcision is illegal in the UK.
3. The Human Rights Act 1988 incorporated the European Convention on Human Rights into UK law.
4. Britain has a long history of respecting an individual's rights and ensuring essential freedoms.

Taxation

1. If you are employed your employer typically deducts income tax through a system called PAYE
2. People who are self-employed need to pay National Insurance contributions themselves.
3. Money raised from income tax pays for government services such as roads, education, police and the armed forces.
4. The money raised from National Insurance Contributions is used to pay for state benefits and services such as the state retirement pension and the National Health Service (NHS)

Driving

1. Drivers can use their driving licence until they are 70 years old.
2. If you are registered in the UK your car or motorcycle must be registered at the Driver and Vehicle Licensing Authority (DVLA)
3. If your vehicle is more than 3 years old you must take for a Ministry of Transport (MOT) test every year.
4. You must be at least 17 years old to drive a car or motor cycle.

Your role in the community

1. Governors and school boards have an important role in raising school standards.
2. You don't have to tell a canvasser how you intend to vote.
3 Donated blood is used by hospitals to help people with a wide range of injuries and illnesses.
4. Crisis and Shelter are charities to do with the homeless.
5. The National Citizen Service programme gives 16- and 17-year olds the opportunity to enjoy outdoor activities.

Practice Test

The pages that follow contain a practice test. Answers are found on the page that follows the test.

As a reminder, the key points about the real Life in the UK Test are:
- The test contains 24 multiple choice questions in English
- You can listen to the questions using headphones provided by the test centre
- You have 45 minutes to complete the test (about 2 minutes per question)
- The pass mark is 75% (18 questions correct out of 24)

Question 1 - Which TWO British fighter aircraft took part in the Battle of Britain?
  A. Hurricane
  B. Vulcan
  C. Spitfire
  D. Dornier

Question 2 - Is the statement below True or False?
In the English Civil War those who supported the king were called 'Cavaliers'
  A. True
  B. False

Question 3 - Which TWO of the people below are famous British inventors?
  A. Bradley Wiggins
  B. John Logie Baird
  C. Gustav Holst
  D. Frank Whittle

Question 4 - When is Boxing Day?
  A. 24 December
  B. 25 December
  C. 26 December
  D. 27 December

Question 5 - Which of these statements is correct?
   A. Tudor King Henry VIII is famous for breaking away from the Church of Rome and marrying six times.
   B. Tudor King Henry VIII is famous for his successful victory against the French at t scrutinise he battle of Agincourt.

Question 6 - Which of these statements is correct?
   A. You need to be at least 17 years of age to drive a car or motorcycle.
   B. You need to be at least 18 years of age to drive a car or motorcycle.

Question 7 - Which body created the European Convention on Human Rights?
   A. The United Nations
   B. The European Union
   C. The Council of Europe
   D. The North Atlantic Treaty Organisation

Question 8 - Which of these statements is correct?
   A. Today girls leave school, on average with better qualifications than boys
   B. Today girls leave school, on average with poorer qualifications than boys.

Question 9 - In the 2009 citizenship ceremony what proportion of people identified themselves as Christian?
   A. Ten per cent (10%)
   B. Thirty per cent (30%)
   C. Fifty per cent (50%)
   D. Seventy per cent (70%)

Question 10 - Is the statement true below True or False?
Margaret Thatcher was Britain's first woman Prime Minister
   A. True
   B. False

Question 11 - Which of these statements is correct?
   A. In the 1840s there was a famine in Ireland and a million people died.
   B. In the 1970s there was a famine in Ireland and a million people died.

Question 12 - What are the TWO homes of the Prime Minister?
- A. 10 Downing Street
- B. Chequers
- C. 11 Downing Street
- D. Marble Arch

Question 13 - Which TWO scientists developed penicillin into a usable drug?
- A. Clement Attlee
- B. Howard Florey
- C. Ernst Chain
- D. Roald Dahl

Question 14 - St David is the Patron Saint of which country?
- A. Wales
- B. England
- C. Scotland
- D. Northern Ireland

Question 15 - Who chairs debates in the House of Commons?
- A. The Prime Minister
- B. The Speaker
- C. The Chancellor of the Exchequer
- D. The Leader of the Opposition

Question 16 - The Wars of the Roses was fought between which TWO families?
- A. The House of York
- B. The House of Windsor
- C. The House of Lancaster
- D. The House of MacDonald

Question 17 - When did women get the right to vote at 21, the same age as men?
- A. 1857
- B. 1918
- C. 1928
- D. 1960

Question 18 - Which of these statements is correct?
   A. People under 18 are not allowed to participate in the National Lottery
   B. People under 16 are not allowed to participate in the National Lottery

Question 19 - Which of these statements is correct?
   A. William of Orange defeated James II at the Battle of Culloden in Scotland
   B. William of Orange defeated James II at the Battle of the Boyne in Ireland

Question 20 - Is the statement below True or False?
Members of the army are allowed to stand for public office.
   A. True
   B. False

Question 21 - Is the statement below True or False?
Cricket is the UK's most popular sport.
   A. True
   B. False

Question 22 - Is the statement below True or False?
Female genital mutilation is illegal in the UK
   A. True
   B. False

Question 23 - Is the statement below True or False?
The Church of England is a Roman Catholic Church
   A. True
   B. False

Question 24 - Is the statement below True or False
The British Constitution is written down in a single document.
   A. True
   B. False

See the next page for answers to this practice test.

Practice Test answers

Question 1 = A, C
Question 2 = A
Question 3 = B, D
Question 4 = C
Question 5 = A
Question 6 = A
Question 7 = C
Question 8 = A
Question 9 = D
Question 10 = A
Question 11 = A
Question 12 = A, B
Question 13 = B, C
Question 14 = A
Question 15 = B
Question 16 = A,C
Question 17 = C
Question 18 = B
Question 19 = B
Question 20 = B
Question 21 = B
Question 22 = A
Question 23 = B
Question 24 = B

Glossary

This glossary will help readers to understand the meanings of key words that appear in this handbook.

When words may be difficult to understand, an example of use may follow the definition. The word that is bracketed after an entry relates to the particular context in which the word is being defined – for example, arrested (*police*)

A slash / separates different definitions.

AD	Anno Domini – referring to the number of years after the birth of Jesus Christ – used as a time reference
allegiance	Loyalty to something - for example, to a leader, a faith or country
armed forces	The army, navy and air force which defend a country in times of peace and war
arrested (police)	Taken by the police to a police station and made to stay there to answer questions about illegal actions or activity
assault	The criminal act of using physical force against someone – for example hitting someone
bank holiday	A day when most people have an official day off work and many businesses are closed. A bank holiday can also be called a public holiday
baron	A man who has one of the ranks of the British nobility. The title was particularly common during the Middle Ages
BC	Before Christ – referring to the number of years before Jesus Christ was born – used as a time reference
bishop	A senior member of the clergy in the Christian religion, often in charge of the churches in a particular area
boom	A sharp rise in something – very often in business activity or the economy
brutality	Behaviour towards another which is cruel and violent and causes harm
by-election	An election held in a parliamentary constituency or local authority area to fill a vacancy (*see General Election*)

cabinet (government)	A group of senior ministers who are responsible for controlling government policy
casualties (medical)	People who are wounded or killed (for example, in war)
charter (government)	An official written statement which describes the rights and responsibilities of a state and its citizens
chieftain	The leader of a clan in Scotland or Ireland
civil disobedience	The refusal of members of the public to obey laws, often because they want to protest against political issues
civil law	The legal system that deals with disputes between people or groups of people
civil service	The departments within government which manage the business of running the country – people who work for the government can be called civil servants
civil war	A war between groups who live in the same country
clan	A group of people or families who live under the same rule of a chieftain and may be descendants of the same person – a term used traditionally in Scotland
clergy	Religious leaders, used here to describe religious leaders in Christian churches
coalition	A partnership between different political parties
commemorate	Show that something or someone is remembered
conquered	Beaten in battle
constituency	The legal structure of established laws and principles which is used to govern a country
Convention (government)	An agreement between countries about particular rules or behaviour
Criminal law	The legal system that deals with illegal activities
decree (law)	Official order, law or decision
democratic country	A country which is governed by people who are elected by the population to represent them in Parliament
devolution	The passing of power from central government to a particular group of people living in a particular area
dialect	A form of language spoken by a particular group of people living in a particular area
domestic policies	Political decisions that relate to what is happening in a country (as opposed to in another country)

electoral register	The official list of all the people in a country who are allowed to vote in an election
electorate	All the people who are allowed to vote in an election
eligible	Allowed by law
ethnic origin	The country of birth of someone's race or the nationality of someone when they were born/the customs and place from which a person and their family originated (or came from).
executed	Killed as punishment
first past the post	A system of election in which the candidate with the largest number of vote in a particular constituency wins a seat in Parliament
franchise	The right to vote
General Election	An event in which all the citizens of a country who are allowed to vote choose the people they wish to represent them in their government
government policies	Official ideas and beliefs that are agreed by a political party about how to govern the country
guilty	Found by a court to have done something which is illegal
heir	Someone who will legally receive a person's money or possessions after their death. The heir to the throne is the person who will become the next king or queen
house (history)	A family (for example, House of York)
House of Commons	That part of the Houses of Parliament where MPs are elected by the voting public debate political issues
House of Lords	That part of the Houses of Parliament where people who have inherited their places or been chosen by the government debate political issues
household	A home and the people who live in it/ something that relates to a home. (For example, household chores are tasks that are done around the house, such as cleaning and cooking.)
Houses of Parliament	The building in London where the House of Commons and House of Lords meet
illegal	Something which the law does not allow

infrastructure	Structured network that is necessary for successful operation of a business or transport system – for example, roads or railways
innocent (law)	Found by a court not to have done something illegal
judge	The most important official in court. The judge makes sure what happens in court is fair and legal
judiciary	All the judges in a country. Together they are responsible for using the law of the land in the correct way
jury (legal)	People who are chosen to sit in court, listen to information about a crime, and decide if someone is guilty or innocent
legal	Allowed to do so by law
legislative power	The power to make laws
liberty	Freedom
magistrate	A person who acts as a judge in a court case where the crime is not a serious one
marital status	Information about whether a person is single, married, separated or divorced. This is often asked for on official forms.
media, the	All the organisations which give information to the public, ie newspapers, magazines, television, radio and the internet
medieval/Middle Ages	In history, the period between 1066 and about 1500
monarch	The king or queen of a country
national issues	Political problems that can affect everyone who lives in a country
nationalized	Bought and then controlled by central government – relating to an industry service that was previously owned privately
nobility	The people in a country who belong to the highest social class, some of whom may have titles – for example, Lord, Duke, Baron
office, to be in	To be in power in government

opposition	In the House of Commons, the largest political party which is not part of the government is officially known as the opposition
Pale (history)	Part of Ireland governed by the English
party politics	The shared ideas and beliefs of an organised group of politicians
patron saint	A Christian saint who is believed to protect a particular area or group of people
penalty (law)	Punishment for breaking the law
Pope, the	The head of the Roman Catholic Church
practise a religion	Live according to the rules and beliefs of a religion
Prime Minister	The politician who leads the government
prohibit/prohibition	Make something illegal
Proportional representation	A system of election in which political parties are allowed a number of seats in Parliament that represents their share of the total number of votes cast
Protestants	Christians who are not members of the Roman Catholic Church
public house/pub	A place where adults can buy and drink alcohol
Reformation, the	The religious movement in the 16th century that challenged authority of the Pope and established Protestant churches in Europe
refugee	A person who must leave the country where they live, often because of war or for political reasons
residence	The place where someone lives
rival viewpoints	Opinions held by different groups of people
rural	Countryside
scrutinise	Examine all the detail
seat (Parliament)	A constituency
sentence (law)	A punishment imposed by a court
shadow cabinet	Senior MPs of a political party not in government
sheriff (law)	A judge in Scotland

slavery	A system in which people bought and sold other people (slaves) who were forced to work without pay
sonnet	A poem which is 14 lines long and rhymes in a particular way
Speaker, the	The member of the House of Commons who controls the way issues are debated in Parliament
stand for office	Apply to be elected – for example, as an MP or councillor
strike, to go on	Refuse to work in order to protest against something
successor (government)	A person who comes after another and takes over an office or receives some kind of power – for example, a son who becomes king when his father dies is a successor
suspend	To stop something from happening or operating, usually for a short time
terrorism	Violence used by people who want to force a government to do something. The violence is usually random and unexpected, so that no one can feel really safe from it.
The Phone Book	A book which contains names, addresses and phone numbers of organisations, businesses and individuals
theft	The criminal act of stealing something from a person building or place
trade union	An association of workers formed to protect its members
treaty	An official written agreement between countries or governments
uprising	A violent revolt or rebellion against authority
voluntary work	Work which someone does because they want to and which they do for free, ie they do not receive any payment
volunteer	Someone who works for free or who offers to do something without payment (see voluntary work)
war effort	The work people did in order to help the country in any way they could during wartime
Yellow Pages	A book that lists names, addresses and telephone numbers of businesses, services and organisations in an area. Also available online at www.yell.com

People mentioned in the study material

People mentioned	Notes
Julius Caesar	Led failed Roman invasion of Britain 55 BC
Emperor Claudius	Led successful Roman invasion of Britain AD43
Boudicca	Queen of tribal leaders who fought against Romans
Emperor Hadrian	Roman Emperor who built Hadrian's wall
St Patrick	Christian missionary
St Columba	Founded monastery on island of Iona
St Augustine	First Archbishop of Canterbury
King Alfred the Great	Defeated the Vikings
Kenneth MacAlpin	United the north (Scots) under one king
Cnut/Canute	First Danish King
King Harold	Saxon king, died at Battle of Hastings 1066
William the Conqueror/ Duke of Normandy	Led the successful Norman invasion of Britain in 1066 'The Norman Conquest'
King Edward I	Annexed Wales. Built welsh castles.
Robert the Bruce	Scottish King. Defeated English at Battle of Bannockburn
King Henry V	Defeated French at Battle of Agincourt 1415
King John	Signed charter of rights Magna Carta 1215
Geoffrey Chaucer	ca 1400 wrote the Canterbury Tales in English
William Caxton	One of the first book printers
King Richard III	House of York, White rose, Killed at Battle of Bosworth Field in 1485
King Henry VII	Henry Tudor of the House of Lancaster, Red rose became the first Tudor king on his victory at the Battle of Bosworth field
Elizabeth of York	Niece of King Richard III, married by Henry Tudor uniting the houses of York and Lancaster
King Henry VIII	Broke from the Church of Rome and had six wives
Catherine of Aragon	First wife of Henry VIII, Mother of Queen Mary, Divorced.

People mentioned	Notes
Anne Boleyn	*Second wife of Henry VIII, Mother of Queen Elizabeth I, Executed*
Jane Seymour	*Third wife of Henry VIII, Mother of King Edward VI, died shortly after giving birth*
Anne of Cleves	*Fourth wife of Henry VIII, German princess, Divorced*
Catherine Howard	*Fifth wife of Henry VIII, Executed*
Catherine Parr	*Sixth wife of Henry VIII, A widow, outlived him, married again*
King Edward VI	*Protestant, Book of Common Prayer written, died at 15*
Queen Mary I (Bloody Mary)	*Catholic, Persecuted Protestants*
Queen Elizabeth I	*Protestant, re-established Church of England, Defeated Spanish Armada 1588, Executed Mary Queen of Scots*
Mary Stuart (Mary Queen of Scots)	*Queen of Scotland, Gave her throne to her son James VI of Scotland (and I of England.) Executed by Queen Elizabeth I (her cousin)*
Sir Francis Drake	*Circumnavigated the world in the Golden Hind*
William Shakespeare 1564 - 1616	*Poet and playwright.*
James VI and I	*Became king of England, Wales and Ireland but Scotland remained a separate country. King James I bible produced.*
King Charles I	*'Divine Right of Kings', English Civil War, Executed 1649*
Oliver Cromwell	*'Lord Protector' of the English republic - The Commonwealth*
Richard Cromwell	*Son of Oliver Cromwell and 'Lord Protector'*
King Charles II	*Restored to the throne in May 1660*
Sir Christopher Wren	*Architect, Designed St Paul's cathedral*
Samuel Pepys	*Diarist, Wrote about the Great Fire of London*
Sir Edmund Halley	*Predicted return of 'Halley's Comet'*

People mentioned	Notes
Isaac Newton (1643-1727)	Scientific discoveries including that white light is made up of the colours of the rainbow
King James II	Brother of Charles II, Catholic, Deposed.
Mary - daughter of James II	Married to her cousin William of Orange the Protestant ruler of the Netherlands
King William III	Deposed James II in the Glorious Revolution. Reigned jointly with Mary. Agreed to a 'Declaration of Rights', Defeated James II at the Battle of the Boyne in Ireland
The MacDonald's of Glencoe	Massacred by followers of William III for being late in taking an oath of allegiance
Queen Anne	Had no surviving children. Act of Union in 1707 creating United Kingdom of Great Britain.
King George I	German. Chosen by Parliament as Anne's nearest Protestant relative. No English.
Sir Robert Walpole	First Prime Minister
King George II	Succession opposed by Bonnie Prince Charlie
Charles Edward Stuart (Bonnie Prince Charlie)	Grandson of James II, defeated by George II at Battle of Culloden 1746, escaped to Europe
Robert Burns	Scottish poet. Known as 'the bard'
Adam Smith	Developed ideas about economics
David Hume	Human nature ideas relevant to philosophers
James Watt	Work on steam power helped Industrial revolution
Richard Arkwright 1732-92	Improved the Carding machine. Known for the efficient and profitable way he ran his factories
Captain James Cook	Explorer, Mapped coast of Australia
Sake Dean Mahomet 1759-1851	Opened Hindoostane Coffee House, introduced the curry and shampooing.
William Wilberforce	Slavery abolitionist, Member of Parliament
Napoleon	Emperor of France
Admiral Nelson	Died at Battle of Trafalgar on HMS Victory, Commemorated by Nelson's Column in Trafalgar Square, London
Duke of Wellington	Known as the Iron Duke, Defeated Napoleon at Battle of Waterloo, became Prime Minister

People mentioned	Notes
Queen Victoria	*Became queen at 18, Reigned until 1901, Victorian Age*
George and Robert Stephenson	*Pioneered railway engine*
Isambard Kingdom Brunel	*Engineer, built Great Western Railway and Clifton Suspension Bridge*
Florence Nightingale	*Nurse during the Crimean War. Regarded as founder of modern nursing.*
Charles Stuart Parnell	*Advocated 'Home rule' in Ireland*
Emmeline Pankhurst 1858-1928	*Suffragette*
Rudyard Kipling 1865-1936	*Author and poet - The Jungle Book, IF*
Archduke Franz Ferdinand of Austria	*His assassination led to the start of World War I*
Graham Greene	*Writer- including of The Heart of the Matter*
Evelyn Waugh	*Writer - including of Brideshead Revisited*
John Maynard Keynes	*Economist*
Adolf Hitler	*Leader of Germany during World War II*
Winston Churchill	*UK Prime Minister during World War II*
Ernest Rutherford	*Scientist, took part in Manhattan project which developed the atomic bomb*
Alexander Fleming 1881-1955	*Discovered penicillin*
Howard Florey and Ernst Chain	*Turned penicillin into a usable drug*
Clement Attlee	*Labour Prime Minister, introduced Welfare State*
Aneurin (Nye) Bevin	*Minister for Health, Established the NHS*
Harold MacMillan	*Conservative Prime Minister, 'Wind of Change' speech*
William Beveridge 1879-1963	*Beveridge report fighting the five great evils*
R A Butler 1902-82	*Education Act 1944. Introduction of free secondary education in England and Wales*
Dylan Thomas 1914-53	*Welsh poet and writer - 'Under Milk Wood'*

People mentioned	Notes
John Logie Baird 1888-1946	*Inventor of the television*
Sir Robert Watson-Watt	*Developed radar*
Sir Bernard Lovell 1913-2012	*Discoveries in astronomy. Jodrell Bank telescope*
Alan Turing 1912-54	*Mathematician influential in development of computer science*
John Macleod 1876-1935	*Co-discoverer of insulin*
Francis Crick 1916-2004	*Co-discoverer of structure of DNA molecule*
Sir Frank Whittle 1907-96	*Development of the Jet engine*
Sir Christopher Cockerell 1910-99	*Inventor of the hovercraft*
James Goodfellow 1937-	*Invented the cash dispensing ATM*
Sir Robert Edwards 1925- and Patrick Steptoe 1913-88	*World's first 'test tube baby'*
Sir Ian Wilmot 1944 - and Keith Campbell 1954-2012	*Successful cloning of a mammal 'dolly the sheep'*
Sir Peter Mansfield 1933-	*Co-inventor of the MRI (magnetic resonance imaging) scanner*
Sir Tim Berners Lee 1955 -	*Inventor of the World Wide Web*
Mary Peters 1939 -	*Olympic gold pentathlon in 1972*
Margaret Thatcher 1925-2003	*First woman Prime Minister of the UK, Conservative*
John Major	*Conservative Prime Minister, helped establish Northern Ireland peace process*
Ronald Reagan	*President of the USA*
Roald Dahl 1916-90	*Author*
Tony Blair	*Labour Prime Minister, Good Friday Agreement signed in 1998*
David Cameron	*Prime Minister of the Conservative and Liberal Democrat coalition*
St David	*Patron saint of Wales*
St Patrick	*Patron saint of Ireland*

People mentioned	Notes
St George	*Patron saint of England*
St Andrew	*Patron saint of Scotland*
Santa Claus/Father Christmas	*Believed to bring presents on Christmas day*
Guy Fawkes	*Conspirator in the plan to kill King James I with a bomb in the Houses of Parliament*
Sir Roger Bannister 1929-	*First to run a mile in under 4 minutes*
Sir Jackie Stewart 1939-	*Scottish former racing driver*
Bobby Moore 1941-93	*Captain of England football team at 1966 World Cup*
Sir Ian Botham 1955-	*English cricket team captain and record holder*
Jayne Torvill 1957- and Christopher Dean 1958-	*Ice dancing gold at 1984 Olympic games and four consecutive world championships*
Sir Steve Redgrave 1962-	*Olympic rowing 5x gold medalist*
Baroness Tanni Grey-Thompson 1969-	*Paralympic gold medalist*
Dame Kelly Holmes 1970-	*Running gold medalist*
Dame Ellen MacArthur 1976-	*Fastest woman to sail around the world single handed (2004)*
Sir Chris Hoy 1976-	*Scottish cyclist and Olympic gold medalist*
David Weir 1979-	*Paralympian.*
Bradley Wiggins 1980-	*First Briton to win the Tour de France*
Mo Farah 1983-	*British distance runner and Olympic medalist*
Jessica Ennis 1986-	*Heptathlon Olympic gold medalist*
Andy Murray 1987-	*Scottish tennis player*
Ellie Simmonds 1994	*Swimming Paralympian*
Damon Hill	*Formula 1 (Grand Prix) World Champion*
Lewis Hamilton	*Formula 1 (Grand Prix) World Champion*
Jensen Button	*Formula 1 (Grand Prix) World Champion*
Henry Purcell 1659-95	*Organist and composer*
George Frederick Handel 1695-1759	*German born composer - including of 'Water Music' and 'the Messiah'*

179

People mentioned	Notes
Gustav Holst 1874 -1934	*Composer known for 'The Planets'*
Sir Edward Elgar 1857-1934	*Composer known for 'Pomp and Circumstances Marches, No. 1 'Land of Hope and Glory*
Ralph Vaughan Williams 1872-1958	*Composer of music for orchestras and choirs*
Sir William Walton 1872-1958	*Composer known for Facade and Balthazar's Feast*
Benjamin Britten 1913-76	*Composer known for his operas including Peter Grimes and Billy Budd*
Dame Agatha Christie	*Murder mystery author*
Gilbert & Sullivan	*Composers of 'comic operas'*
Andrew Lloyd Webber	*Composer of music shows - eg Evita*
Tim Rice	*collaborator with Andrew Lloyd Webber*
Sir Laurence Olivier	*Shakespearian Actor*
Hans Holbein	*Foreign painter working in Britain*
Sir Anthony Van Dyck	*Foreign painter working in Britain*
Thomas Gainsborough 1727-88	*Portrait painter*
David Allan 1744-96	*Scottish portrait painter*
Joseph Turner 1775-1851	*Landscape painter*
John Constable 1776-1837	*Landscape painter*
Sir John Lavery 1856-1941	*Northern Irish portrait painter*
Henry Moore 1898-1986	*English sculptor*
John Petts 1914-91	*Welsh artist working with stained glass*
Lucian Freud 1922-2011	*German born British artist. Portraits.*
David Hockney 1937-	*Contributor to 'pop art' movement of 1960s*
Damien Hurst	*winner of Turner prize*
Richard Wright	*winner of Turner prize*
Robert Adam	*Scottish Architect - including Dumfries House*
Sir Edwin Lutyens	*Architect - including the Cenotaph*
Sir Norman Foster	*Modern British architect*
Lord (Richard) Rogers	*Modern British architect*

People mentioned	Notes
Dame Zaha Hadid	*Modern British architect*
Lancelot 'Capability' Brown	*18th century landscape gardener*
Gertrud Jekyll	*18th century landscape gardener*
Thomas Chippendale	*18th century furniture designer*
Clarice Cliff	*Art Deco ceramic designer*
Sir Terence Conran	*20th century interior designer*
Mary Quant	*Fashion designer*
Alexander McQueen	*Fashion designer*
Vivienne Westwood	*Fashion designer*
Sir William Golding	*Novelist and winner of Nobel prize for literature*
Seamus Heaney	*Poet and winner of Nobel prize for literature*
Harold Pinter	*Playwright and winner of Nobel prize for literature*
Ian Fleming	*Author of James Bond books*
JRR Tolkien	*Author of 'Lord of the Rings' and 'The Hobbit'*
Ian McEwan	*Past winner of Man Booker Prize for Fiction*
Hilary Mantel	*Past winner of Man Booker Prize for Fiction*
Julian Barnes	*Past winner of Man Booker Prize for Fiction*
Jane Austen 1775-1817	*Author - 'Pride and Prejudice'*
Charles Dickens 1812-70	*Author - 'Great Expectations'*
Robert Louis Stevenson 1850-94	*Author - 'Treasure Island'*
Thomas Hardy 1840-1928	*Author - 'Far from the Madding Crowd'*
Sir Arthur Conan Doyle 1859-1930	*Scottish doctor and writer - 'Sherlock Holmes' stories*
Evelyn Waugh 1903-66	*Author of satirical novels - 'Decline and Fall'*
Sir Kinglsey Amis 1922-95	*English novelist and poet - 'Lucky Jim'*
Graham Greene 1904-91	*Author - 'The Heart of the Matter'*
JK Rowling 1965-	*Author - 'The Harry Potter series'*
John Milton	*Protestant poet - 'Paradise lost'*
William Wordsworth	*Poet - 'The daffodils'*
Sir Walter Scott	*Poems inspired by Scotland*

People mentioned	Notes
William Blake	*19th century poet - 'The Tyger'*
John Keats	*19th century poet*
Lord Byron	*19th century poet - 'She walks in beauty'*
Percy Shelley	*19th century poet*
Alfred Lord Tennyson	*19th century poet*
Robert Browning	*19th century poet - 'Home thoughts from abroad'*
Elizabeth Browning	*19th century poet*
Wilfred Owen	*First World War poet - 'Anthem for Doomed Youth'*
Siegfried Sassoon	*First World War poet*
Sir Walter de la Mare	*More recent popular poet*
John Masefield	*More recent popular poet*
Sir John Betjeman	*More recent popular poet*
Ted Hughes	*More recent popular poet*
Carol Reed	*Film director - The Third Man*
Sir Alexander Korda	*Film director - Brief Encounter*
Sir Alfred Hitchcock	*Film director - The 39 Steps*
Sir David Lean	*Film director - Lawrence of Arabia*
Ridley Scott	*Film director*
Frank Launder	*Film director - The Belle's of St Trinians*
Ken Russell	*Film director - Women in Love*
Nicolas Roeg	*Film director - Don't Look Now*
Hugh Hudson	*Film director - Chariots of Fire*
Roland Joffe	*Film director - The Killing Fields*
Mike Newell	*Film director - Four Weddings and a Funeral*
Kevin MacDonald	*Film director - Touching the Void*
Sir Charles (Charlie) Chaplin	*Silent movie actor*
David Niven	*Actor*
Sir Rex Harrison	*Actor*
Richard Burton	*Actor*
Colin Firth	*Oscar winning British actor*
Sir Anthony Hopkins	*Oscar winning British actor*

People mentioned	Notes
Pre-Raphaelites	Artists Holman Hunt, Rossetti and John Millais
Dame Judi Dench	Oscar winning British actor
Kate Winslet	Oscar winning British actor
Tilda Swinton	Oscar winning British actor
Morecambe and Wise	Comedians
Queen Elizabeth II	The Queen - Current monarch
Prince Philip	Duke of Edinburgh and husband of the Queen
Prince Charles	Prince of Wales, son of the Queen and heir to the throne

Conflicts mentioned in the study material

Conflicts mentioned	Notes
The Crusades	Christians fight for control of the Holy Land
The Hundred Years War	War with France
The Wars of the Roses	House of Lancaster v House of York
The English Civil War	Royalists versus Parliamentarians
The Glorious Revolution	James II deposed by William III
The Rebellion of the Clans	Bonnie Prince Charlie defeated by George II at Culloden
The American War of Independence	Colonists defeat British Army
The French Wars	End with defeat of Napoleon at Waterloo
The Crimean War	Britain fought with Turkey and France against Russia
The Boer War	Britain fought settlers in South Africa from the Netherlands
The First World War	Allied powers (including Britain) fought against the Central powers (including Germany)
The Easter Rising	Rebellion in Ireland against British rule

Conflicts mentioned	Notes
Guerilla war in Ireland	*Followed execution of leaders of the Easter Rising by the British*
The Second World War	*The Allies (including Britain) fought against the Axis powers (including Germany and Japan)*
The Falklands War	*British forces recaptured the Falkland Islands from Argentina*
Liberation of Kuwait	*Iraqi forces expelled from Kuwait by a coalition including Britain*
Conflict in former Yugoslavia	*Involvement of British forces*
Operations in Iraq	*Involvement of British forces*
Afghanistan	*Involvement of British forces as part of International Security Assistance Force (ISAF)*

Battles mentioned in the study material

Battles mentioned	Notes
Battle of Hastings 1066	*Normans led by William the Conqueror defeat Saxons. Death of Saxon King Harold. Commemorated in Bayeux Tapestry*
Battle of Bannockburn 1314	*Scottish led by King Robert the Bruce defeats the English army of Edward II*
Battle of Agincourt 1415	*Part of the Hundred Years War. Henry V's vastly outnumbered army defeated the French.*
Battle of Bosworth Field 1485	*King Richard III of the House of York (white rose) killed in battle by the forces of Henry Tudor of the House of Lancaster (red rose). Henry Tudor became King Henry VII*
Spanish Armada 1588	*English defeated a fleet of ships sent from Spain*
Battle of Marston Moor 1644	*King Charles I army defeated by Parliamentarian forces*

Battles mentioned	Notes
Battle of Naseby 1645	*King Charles I army defeated by Parliamentarian forces*
Battle of Dunbar 1650	*Cromwell defeats Scottish army of Charles II*
Battle of Worcester 1651	*Cromwell defeats Scottish army of Charles II*
Battle of Killiecrankie 1689	*Jacobite rising in support of James II. Scottish clans defeat forces loyal to William III (note - the study materials say that the Scots were defeated but this is incorrect)*
Battle of the Boyne 1690	*King James II defeated by William of Orange*
Battle of Culloden 1746	*Jacobite forces of Charles Edward Stuart (Bonnie Prince Charlie), the grandson of James II, defeated by George II's army*
Battle of Trafalgar 1805	*British fleet defeat a combined Napoleonic French and Spanish fleet. Horatio Nelson killed.*
Battle of Waterloo 1815	*Defeat of Emperor Napoleon by Duke of Wellington*
Battle of the Somme 1916	*First World War - British offensive on German defences. 60,000 British casualties in one day*
Dunkirk 1940	*Second World War - Evacuation of 300,000 men from the beaches around Dunkirk, France*
Battle of Britain 1940	*Second World War - aerial battle against the Germans*
Blitz 1940/41	*Second World War - German air campaign against Britain*
Pearl Harbor 1941	*Second World War - Japanese bombing attack on US Naval base*
D-Day 1944	*Second World War - Allied landings in Normandy*

Annual calendar events mentioned in the study material

Calendar event	Date
New Year's Day	1 January
Valentine's Day	14 February
St David's Day	1 March
St Patrick's Day	17 March
April Fool's Day	1 April
Vaisakhi (also spelled Baisakhi)	14 April
St George's Day	23 April
D-day landings anniversary	6 June
Battle of the Boyne anniversary (Northern Ireland only)	12 July
Halloween	31 October
Bonfire Night	5 November
Remembrance Day	11 November
St Andrew's Day	30 November
Christmas Eve	24 December
Christmas Day	25 December
Boxing Day	26 December
New Year's Eve (Hogmanay in Scotland)	31 December
Lent	Starts 20 days before Easter
Mothering Sunday	Sunday 3 weeks before Easter
Shrove Tuesday (Pancake day)	The day before Easter starts
Easter	March or April
Father's day	3rd Sunday in June
Diwali	October or November
Hannukah	November or December
Eid- al Fitr	Varies
Eid- ul Adha	Varies

Legislation and documents
mentioned in the study material

Legislation and documents	Notes
Domesday book	*Survey of England completed for William the Conqueror*
Magna Carta 1215	*Limits to the power of King John*
Statute of Rhuddlan 1284	*Annexation of Wales by King Edward I*
Acts for the Government of Wales 1536 and 1543	*Formal union of Wales and England during reign of Henry VIII*
The Habeas Corpus Act 1679	*Charles II. Act guarantees that no one can be held prisoner unlawfully*
The Bill of Rights 1689	*William & Mary. Act confirmed rights of Parliament and limits of the king's power*
Act of Union (or Treaty of Union in Scotland) 1707	*Queen Anne. Created Kingdom of Great Britain*
Act of Union 1800	*Ireland became unified with England, Scotland and Wales to create the United Kingdom of England, Scotland, Wales and Ireland I*
1807	*Ilegal to trade slaves from British ships or ports*
Reform Act 1832	*Increased number of people who could vote and abolished 'pocket' and 'rotten boroughs'*
Emancipation Act 1833	*Abolished slavery in British Empire*
Repeal of the Corn Laws 1846	*Abolishment of import taxes on some goods*
1847	*Working hours for women and children limited by law to 10 per day*
Reform Act 1867	*Created more urban seats in Parliament and reduced the amount of property that people needed before they could vote*

Legislation and documents	Notes
Acts of Parliament in 1872 and 1882	*Gave wives the right to keep their own earnings and property on marriage*
Home Rule Bill introduced 1913	*Proposal for devolved government in Ireland opposed by Protestants and postponed with the start of World War I*
1918	*Women over 30 gain voting rights*
Peace treaty 1921	*Ireland became two countries*
1928	*Women given right to vote at 21 - the same age as men*
The Education Act 1944 (Butler Act)	*Free secondary education in England and Wales*
Beveridge Report 1948	*Outlined Welfare State*
European Convention on Human Rights and Fundamental Freedoms 1950	*Convention signed by UK in 1950*
1960s	*Laws giving women the right to equal pay and making it illegal for employers to discriminate against women because of their gender*
The Belfast (or Good Friday) Agreement 1998	*Northern Ireland peace process*
The Human Rights Act 1998	*Incorporated the European Convention on Human Rights and Fundamental Freedoms into UK law*
The electoral register	*List of all those eligible to vote*
Hansard	*Captures the Proceedings of Parliament*
Forced Marriage (Civil Protection) Act 2007 [2011 in Scotland]	*Court orders can protect a person against forced marriage*

Historical timeline for the UK based on the study material

Period	Monarch	Year	Notes
Stone Age		*10000 years ago*	
		6000 years ago	*First farmers arrive in Britain*
Bronze Age		*4000 years ago*	*People learned to make Bronze*
Iron Age	*Iron Age kings*	*after the Bronze Age*	*Beginnings of British history*
Roman Empire		*55 BC*	*Invasion by Julius Caesar fails*
		AD43	*Successful invasion by Emperor Claudius*
		3rd and 4th centuries AD	*First Christian communities appear in Britain*
		AD 410	*Roman army leaves Britain*
Anglo Saxon		*AD 600*	*Anglo-Saxon kingdoms established in Britain*
		AD 789	*First Viking raiders*
	King Alfred the Great		*Defeated the Vikings in England*
	Kenneth McAlpin		*Defeated the Vikings in the North*
	Cnut		*A Danish king*
	Harold		*Saxon king defeated by William I*

Period	Monarch	Year	Notes
Norman Conquest	*William I*	*1066*	*William, Duke of Normandy, becomes William I after defeating king Harold at the Battle of Hastings*
			Last successful foreign invasion of England
			Scots and Welsh repel Norman invaders
			Bayeux tapestry
			Domesday book
The Middle Ages		*1066-1485*	
13th century		*1200*	*English rule 'the Pale' around Dublin, Ireland*
			Start of The Crusades - series of Christian military campaigns to recapture 'the Holy Land'
	John	*1215*	*Magna Carta*
	Edward I	*1284*	*Annexation of Wales (Statute of Rhuddlan). Castle building in Wales*
14th century	*Edward II**	*1314*	*English defeated at Battle of Bannockburn by Robert the Bruce of Scotland*
	Edward III*	*1348*	*The Black Death - plague*
15th century	*Richard II**	*by 1400*	*Official documents now in English. First book printing by Caxton, Chaucer's Canterbury tales published.*
	Henry V	*1415*	*Hundred Years War. Henry V is victorious against the French at the Battle of Agincourt*
	Henry VI*	*1450*	*English leave France*
		by mid 15th century	*Welsh rebellions defeated*

Period	Monarch	Year	Notes
		1455	*Wars of the Roses for control of the crown between Houses of York and Lancaster.*
	Richard III	*1485*	*End of War of the Roses. King Richard III (Yorkist) killed in Battle of Bosworth field with Henry Tudor (Lancastrian) becoming King Henry VII*
The Tudors			
16th century	*Henry VII*		*Strengthened central administration and reduced power of nobles*
	Henry VIII	*21 April 1509*	*Henry VIII becomes king*
The Reformation			*The Reformation - movement against the authority of the Catholic Pope leading to Protestant churches. Church of England established.*
	Edward VI	*28 Jan 1547*	*Death of Henry VIII. Protestant Edward VI becomes king. Dies aged 15 having ruled for 6 years*
	Mary I	*1553*	*Catholic 'Bloody' Mary becomes queen. Known for persecution of Protestants*
Elizabethan period	*Elizabeth I*	*1560*	*Reformation in Scotland. Protestant church of Scotland established. Authority of Pope and Catholic services made illegal*
		1558	*Spanish Armada defeated*
		1587	*Mary Stuart 'Queen of Scots' executed*
The Stuarts			
17th century	*James I (and VI of Scotland)*	*1603*	*Elizabeth's cousin becomes James I of England, Wales and Ireland and VI of Scotland*

Period	Monarch	Year	Notes
The Stuarts ***The English Civil War***	*Charles I*	*1640*	*Imposition of a revised prayer book in Scotland leads to serious unrest. Parliament refuses to give Charles I money to raise an army even after Scotland invades.*
		1641	*Cromwell suppresses a revolt in Ireland and establishes authority of Parliament*
		1642	*Civil war between King and Parliament*
	Parliament	*1646*	*Charles I army defeated at Marston Moor and Naseby. Clear that Parliament had won the war. Charles held as prisoner.*
	Parliament	*1649*	*Charles I executed*
	Oliver Cromwell	*1653-1658*	*Oliver Cromwell rules as 'Lord Protector' until his death.*
		1656	*First Jews settle in London since Middle Ages*
	Richard Cromwell	*1658-1660*	*Oliver Cromwell's son Richard rules as 'Lord Protector' but lacks authority*
The Restoration	*Charles II*	*May 1660*	*Charles II returns from exile in the Netherlands*
		1665	*Major outbreak of plague in London*
		1666	*Great Fire of London*
		1679	*Habeas Corpus Act becomes law*
		1680 - 1720	*Huguenot refugees from France*

Period	Monarch	Year	Notes
	James II (and VII of Scotland)	*1685*	*Charles II's catholic brother becomes king*
The Glorious Revolution	*William III and Mary*	*1688*	*James II deposed by William of Orange. 'Glorious' because there was no fighting in England. William rules jointly with his wife - James II's elder daughter*
		1689	*Bill of Rights. Monarch must be Protestant.*
		1690	*William III defeats James II at the Battle of the Boyne in Ireland*
The Enlightenment *18th century*	*Anne*	*1707*	*Act of Union creates Kingdom of Great Britain*
	George I	*1714*	*Anne's nearest Protestant relative. German*
		1721	*First Prime Minister - Sir Robert Walpole*
	George II	*1745*	*Charles Edward Stuart (Bonnie Prince Charlie), grandson of James II, attempts to depose George II*
	George II	*1746*	*Battle of Culloden. Bonnie Prince Charlie defeated by army loyal to George II*
The Industrial Revolution	*George III**	*1776*	*American War of Independence starts*
		1783	*American independence recognised. Colonists defeat British army*

Period	Monarch	Year	Notes
		1789	*Revolution in France. French government declares war on Britain. Napoleon becomes emperor of France and continues the war*
		1801	*Act of Union creates United Kingdom of England, Scotland, Wales and Ireland. Union Flag created.*
		21 October 1805	*Battle of Trafalgar, French and Spanish fleets defeated. Admiral Nelson killed in battle on HMS Victory*
19th century		1807	*Made illegal to trade slaves in British ships or ports*
		1815	*French wars end with defeat of Napoleon by Duke of Wellington at Waterloo*
	William IV*	1832	*First Reform Act increases number of people who can vote and abolishes rotten and pocket boroughs*
		1830s/40s	*Chartists campaign for reform*
		1833	*Emancipation Act abolishes slavery across British Empire*
Victorian Age	*Victoria*	1837	*Victoria becomes Queen aged 18*
		1846	*Corn Laws repealed*
		1847	*Law limits number of hours that women and children can work to 10 a day*
		1851	*Great Exhibition opened in Hyde Park in the Crystal Palace*

Period	Monarch	Year	Notes
Victorian Age		*1853-1856*	*Crimean War. Britain fought with Turkey and France against Russia*
		1853	*Women's Franchise League founded by Emmeline Pankhurst which fought to get the vote in elections for married women*
		1861	*Migration as a result of the potato famine in Ireland leads to large Irish populations in cities such as London, Liverpool, Manchester and Glasgow*
		1867	*Second Reform Act creates more urban seats in Parliament and reduces the amount of property needed before men could vote.*
		1870 and 1882	*Acts of Parliament give wives the right to keep their own earnings and property*
		1872	*First Tennis club founded at Leamington Spa*
		1889-1902	*Boer War. British army defeats settlers from the Netherlands in South Africa. The war made questions about the future of the empire more urgent.*
		1895	*The National Trust founded*
20th century		*1901*	*Queen Victoria dies after almost 46 years on the throne*
The Edwardian Period**		*1902*	*Motor-car racing starts in the UK*
	Edward VII*	*1903*	*Women's Social and Political Union founded. Members were called suffragettes*

Period	Monarch	Year	Notes
		1908	Olympic games hosted
	George V*	1913	Home Rule Bill for Ireland introduced
The First World War *1914-1918*		28 Jun 1914	Archduke Franz Ferdinand of Austria assassinated setting in motion the chain of events that leads to World War One
		Jul 1916	The Battle of the Somme. 60,000 British casualties on first day
		1916	Easter Rising in Ireland. Failed revolt by Irish nationalists. Leaders executed.
		11 Nov 1918	First World War ends at 11am with victory for Britain and its allies
The inter war period		1918	Women over the age of 30 given voting rights and the right to stand for Parliament
		1921	Following a guerilla war in Ireland a peace treaty is signed.
		1922	Ireland becomes two countries. Six counties in the north remain part of the UK under the name Northern Ireland
		1922	Northern Ireland Parliament established
		1922	BBC starts radio broadcasts
		1928	Women gain the right to vote at the age of 21 - the same as men

Period	Monarch	Year	Notes
		1933	*Adolf Hitler came to power in Germany*
	George VI*	*1936*	*BBC begins world's first regular TV service*
The Second World War		*1939*	*Hitler's Germany invades Poland. Britain and France declare war.*
		1940	*Winston Churchill becomes Prime Minister*
		1940	*German forces defeat allied troops and advance through France. Evacuation of 300,000 men from the beaches around Dunkirk*
		Summer 1940	*Battle of Britain. Royal Air Force win crucial air battle. This was followed by 'The Blitz' a German bombing campaign.*
		June 1940 to June 1941	*Britain and the Empire stood almost alone against Nazi Germany until the German invasion of the Soviet Union in June 1941*
		Dec 1941	*The US enters the war following the Japanese bombing of Pearl Harbor*
		1942	*Beveridge report published*
		1944	*Introduction of free secondary school education (Butler Act)*
		6 Jun 1944	*D-day Allied landings in Normandy*
		May 1945	*Allies defeat Germany*

Period	Monarch	Year	Notes
		August 1945	*Japan surrenders to the allies following the dropping of atomic bombs on Hiroshima and Nagasaki*
Post war Britain		*1945*	*United Nations founded*
		1945	*Labour government elected. Clement Attlee Prime Minister establishes The Welfare State*
		1947	*Independence given to nine countries including India, Pakistan and Ceylon (Sri Lanka)*
		1947-1967	*Other colonies in Africa, Caribbean and Pacific achieve independence*
		1948	*Olympic games hosted*
		1948	*Workers from West Indies invited to come and work in UK*
		1948	*Aneurin Bevan establishes NHS*
		1950	*UK is one of the first to sign the European Convention on Human Rights and Fundamental Freedoms*
		1951-1964	*Period of Conservative government (Winston Churchill and Harold MacMillan mentioned)*
	Elizabeth II	*1952*	*Queen Elizabeth II becomes queen*
		1957	*West Germany, France, Belgium, Italy, Luxembourg and the Netherlands form the EEC*

Period	Monarch	Year	Notes
		1958	*Power of Prime Minister to nominate peers for their own lifetime - Life peers*
Swinging Sixties		*1960s*	*Social laws liberalised - especially those relating to divorce, abortion, gender discrimination and equal pay.*
		1960s	*New laws introduced restricting immigration*
		1966	*England's football team win the World Cup*
		1969	*Voting age for men and women reduced to 18*
1970s and the 'Troubles' in Northern Ireland		*1970s*	*'The Troubles'. Unrest and terror campaigns in Northern Ireland which began in 1969 between those seeking full Irish independence and those wishing to remain part of the UK*
		1972	*Northern Ireland Parliament abolished*
		1973	*UK joins the EEC (now EU)*
The 'Thatcher' government		*1979*	*Conservative government under the first women Prime Minister - Margaret Thatcher*
		1982	*Falklands War - a UK 'task force' recaptures the islands from Argentina*
The 'Major' government		*1990*	*Conservative government under John Major who helps establish the Northern Ireland peace process*

Period	Monarch	Year	Notes
The 'Blair' government		*1997*	*Labour government under Prime Minister Tony Blair*
		1998	*Belfast (Good Friday) Agreement leads to 'peace in Northern Ireland' and establishment of the Northern Ireland Assembly*
		1998	*Human Rights Act incorporates the European Convention on Human Rights and Fundamental freedoms into UK law*
		1999	*Hereditary peers lose automatic right to attend the House of Lords*
		1999	*First Northern Ireland Assembly, Welsh Assembly and Scottish government are formed*
		Since 2000	*British forces engaged in 'global fight against terrorism and proliferation of weapons of mass destruction', including operations in Kuwait, Iraq, Afghanistan and the former Republic of Yugoslavia*
The 'Brown' government		*2007*	*Labour government under Gordon Brown*
		2009	*British combat troops leave Iraq*
'Coalition' government		*May 2010*	*Coalition government under David Cameron (Conservative) with the Liberal Democrats*
		2012	*London hosts Olympic and Paralympic games*
		Nov 2012	*Public elected 'Police and Crime Commissioners'*
		2012	*Queen Elizabeth II's Diamond Jubilee*

* King's marked with an asterix (*) are not mentioned in the study materials.
** The Edwardian period is not mentioned in the study guide.

Image credits

A1 Grand Prix © Tan Kian Khoon
Horse racing © Number 876085
TV Aerial © Number 1972054
Cricket Match © Number 2779017
Steam Engine Wheels © Number 3878376
World War I bi-planes © Number415368
British Redcoats © Number 4661555
Eden Project © Picasa 2.6n
The Prioress and the Knight from The
Canterbury Tales by Geoffrey Chaucer - Woodcut
from the Caxton's Edition of 1485
© Number 10912986
Union Jack © Number 12889397
Isolated Spitfire © Gary Scott 19671706
Two British Police Constables in uniform
standing together © Howard Sayer London
Olympic Stadium Construction Site at Night ©
Number 24545106
Adam Smith Monument © Number 30907009
Union Jack on Flagpole © Diego Barbieri
John Milton (1608-1674) on engraving from
the 1800s. Engraved by O. Cook and published
by William Mackenzie. © Number 32216632
William Wordsworth (1770-1850) on engraving
from 1846. Engraved by J.Cochran after a
painting by W.Boxall and published by Fisher,
Son & Co, London. © Number 32221633
William Shakespeare © Number 33658841
Tutor © Keith Spalding
Rugby © Number 41620270
Hovercraft © Number 41956127
Motorway traffic © Number 42384469
Man with clenched fist and woman cowering
© Number 42590805
Welsh Cakes © MNL
Easter Eggs © Erick Nguyen
London Eye © Number 51387941
Winter in Snowdonia © Number 51476744
Man in Scanner © Number 53156310
The church of Saint James, Avebury, England
© Number 53471243
United Kingdom of Great Britain and Northern
Ireland (British flag) on the map of Europe
© Number 54342990
HM Revenue and Customs © Number 54386412

Tower of London © Number 55949350
Henry Moore Sculpture © Number 57129981
Classical music concert © Number 57235523
ATM © Number 59896391
Music concert © Number 60329071
Round bookshelf in public library
© Number 61288726
Breakfast in Northern Ireland, Ulster Fry
©Joerg Beuge
'Global Network © Number 63334081
Jalfrezi with rice © Number 63996298
British Money Notes © Maj Seda
Ben Nevis © Number 64969300
London Mosque © Number 66020571
Praying pilgrim in Amritsar © Number
66043440
Dylan Thomas statue © Number 66351059
Thistles © Scisetti Alfio
Arabic tea, rosary and dates © Karaidel
Signing legal document © Number 66778551
England circulating coins © Number 67188753
Edinburgh castle © Number 67309611
Scales of Justice, Old Bailey © Keith Mindham
Photogtraphy
Social media icons © Number 67898005
Young woman pouring drink in pub
©Nigel Spooner
EU flag in front of Berlaymont building façade
© Number 68767205
Sea Harrier Jump Jet - isolated on white
© Number 68975649
Studio Portrait of Three Women Wearing
Volunteer T Shirts © Graham Oliver
Sailing in a gale ©Alexander Nikiforov
Santa is placing gift boxes under Christmas tree
© Kirill Kedrinskiy
Diwali Lamps © Nikhil Gangavane
The Globe Theatre © Number 73429667
Sunset at Giant's Causeway © Aitor Muñoz
Muñoz at Dollar Photo Club
Man taking roast turkey out of the oven
© Monkey Business Images
Daffodil flower or narcissus isolated on white
background cutout © Number 74255197
Lord Byron (1788-1824) on engraving from
1873. Engraved by unknown artist and published
in ''Portrait Gallery of Eminent Men and
Women with Biographies'',USA,1873. © Number
74446118
Walter Scott (1771-1832) Engraved by unknown
artist. Published in ''Portrait Gallery of Eminent
Men and Women with Biographies'',USA,1873
© Number 74448083

Plague Doctors https://commons.wikimedia. org/wiki/Category:Plague_doctors#/media/ File:Doktorschnabel_430px.jpg The original uploader was Drop-atom at English Wikibooks [Public domain], via Wikimedia Commons

Elizabeth I formerly attributed to George Gower https://commons.wikimedia.org/wiki/ File:Elizabeth_I_(Armada_Portrait).jpg Open Government Licence V3 (http://www. nationalarchives.gov.uk/doc/open-government-licence/version/3/), via Wikimedia Commons

Francis Drake by Marcus Gheeraerts the Younger https://commons.wikimedia.org/wiki/ File:1590_or_later_Marcus_Gheeraerts,_Sir_ Francis_Drake_Buckland_Abbey,_Devon.jpg [Public domain], via Wikimedia Commons

David Cameron – From Past Prime Ministers portraits https://www.gov.uk/government/history/ past-prime-ministers Open Government Licence V3 (http://www.nationalarchives.gov.uk/doc/ open-government-licence/version/3/)

Past Prime Ministers portraits. The official photographs of previous Prime Ministers https://www.gov.uk/government/history/past-prime-ministers Open Government Licence V3 (http://www.nationalarchives.gov.uk/doc/open-government-licence/version/3/)

Edward VI. Scanned from Hearn, Karen, ed. Dynasties: Painting in Tudor and Jacobean England 1530-1630. New York: Rizzoli, 1995. ISBN 0-8478-1940-X. https://commons. wikimedia.org/wiki/File:Edward_VI_of_ England_c._1546.jpg via Wikimedai commons

Queen Mary by Antonis Mor https://commons. wikimedia.org/wiki/File:Anthonis_Mor_-_ Queen_Mary_Tudor_of_England_-_WGA16178. jpg [Public domain], via Wikimedia Commons

Globe Theatre by Wenceslas Hollar derivative work: Old Moonraker (This file was derived from: The Old Globe.jpg) https://commons. wikimedia.org/wiki/File:Hollar_Long_View_ detail.png [Public domain], via Wikimedia Commons

*Battle of Worcester by Machell Stace https:// commons.wikimedia.org/wiki/File:Battle_*

of_Worcester.jpg [CC BY-SA 2.5 (http:// creativecommons.org/licenses/by-sa/2.5)], via Wikimedia Commons

Whigs and Tories. From clker.com, The Tories and the Whigs pulling for a crown: PC 3 - 1789--Tories and the Whigs LC-DIG-ppmsca-04313. No known restrictions on publication.

Richard Arkwright – Carding machine From the official Life in the UK Test Study Guide – Open Government Licence V3 (http://www. nationalarchives.gov.uk/doc/open-government-licence/version/3/)

Sake Dean Mahomet. From the book cover of An Eighteenth-Century Journey Through India (held British Library).

Fall of Nelson. As reproduced in the Official Life in the UK Test Study Guide. Open Government Licence V3 (http://www.nationalarchives.gov.uk/ doc/open-government-licence/version/3/), https:// commons.wikimedia.org/wiki/Category:Death_ of_Horatio_Nelson#/media/File:Fall_of_Nelson. jpg, By Denis Dighton [Public domain], via Wikimedia Commons

British Empire map 1921 https://commons. wikimedia.org/wiki/File:British_Empire.png restriction free, via Wiki Commons

The Battle of Culloden. Oil on canvas, David Morier,1746 Public Domain https://commons. wikimedia.org/wiki/File:The_Battle_of_ Culloden.jpg?uselang=en-gb via Wikimedia Commons

Chartist riot. Engraving from 1886 book "True Stories of the Reign of Queen Victoria" by Cornelius Brown. https://commons.wikimedia. org/wiki/File:ChartistRiot.jpg?uselang=en-gb Public Domain, via Wikimedia Commons

Sufragettes.Wiki Common (WSPU leaders Annie Kenney (left) and Christabel Pankhurst}} |Source http://www.hastingspress.co.uk/history/sufpix. htm Author =unknown, Date =c1908 - no known copyright restrictions, via Wikimedia Commons

Emmeline Pankhurst. This image is available from the United States Library of Congress's

---

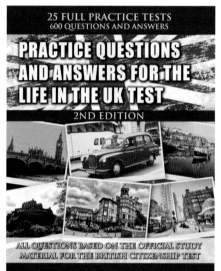